TEACHER'S PET PUBLICATIONS

PUZZLE PACK
for
Things Fall Apart

based on the book by
Chinua Achebe

Written by
William T. Collins

© 2005 Teacher's Pet Publications
All Rights Reserved

The materials in this packet are copyrighted
by Teacher's Pet Publications, Inc.

These pages may be duplicated by the purchaser
for use in the purchaser's own classroom.

Copying any of these materials and distributing them
for any other purpose is a violation of the copyright laws.

© 2005 Teacher's Pet Publications, Inc.
www.tpet.com

INTRODUCTION
If you already own the LitPlan for this title, this Puzzle Pack will refresh your Unit Resource Materials and Vocabulary Resource Materials sections plus give you additional materials you can substitute into the tests. If you do not already have a complete LitPlan, these pages will give you some supplemental materials to use with your own plan. There are two main groups of materials: one set for unit words (such as characters' names, symbols, places, etc.) and one set for vocabulary words associated with the book.

WORD LIST
There is a word list for both the unit words and the vocabulary words. These lists show you which words are being used in the materials and the clues or definitions being used for those words. You may want to give students a word list with clues/definitions to help them, or you may want students to only have a word list (without clues/definitions) if you want them to work a little harder. Both are available for duplication. The word lists can also be your "calling key" for the bingo games.

FILL IN THE BLANK AND MATCHING
There are 4 each of the fill in the blank and matching worksheets for both the unit and vocabulary words. These pages can be used either as extra worksheets for students or as objective parts of a unit test. They can be done individually if students need extra help or as a whole class activity to review the material covered.

MAGIC SQUARES
The magic squares not only reinforce the material covered but also work on reasoning and math skills. Many teachers have told us that their students really enjoy doing these!

WORD SEARCH PUZZLES
The word search words go in all directions, as indicated on your answer keys. Two of the word search puzzles have the clues listed rather than the words. This makes the puzzle a little more difficult, but it reinforces the material better. Two word search puzzles have words only for students who find the clue puzzles too difficult.

CROSSWORD PUZZLES
Both unit and vocabulary word sections have 4 crossword puzzles.

BINGO CARDS
There are 32 individual bingo cards for the unit words and 32 individual bingo cards for the vocabulary words. You can use your word list as a "call list," calling the words at random and marking them off of your list as you go, or you could use the flash cards by cutting them apart and drawing the words at random from a hat (or box or whatever). To make a better review, you might ask for the definition and spelling of each word as you call it out–or you could call out the definitions and have students tell you the words they need to look for on the puzzle.

JUGGLE LETTERS
The vocabulary juggle letter game is intended to help students learn the spellings of the words. One sheet has the definitions listed on it as an extra help for students who need it or to reinforce the definitions if you choose to do so.

FLASH CARDS
We've included a set of vocabulary flash cards you can duplicate, cut, and fold for your students. Some teachers make a few sets for general use by the class; others make a set for each student. Some teachers duplicate them for each student and have the students cut & fold their own. You can cut out just the words and put them in a hat, have each student pick out one word and write the definition and a sentence for that word. Students then swap words and papers, with the next student adding a sentence of his own under the last one. You can have students swap as many times as you like. Each time the student will read the sentences written prior to his own and then add a sentence. You can cut out the words and definitions separately and play "I Have; Who Has?" Each student in the room draws a word and definition. The first student says, "I have (the name of the word). Who has the definition?" The student with the definition reads it then says, "I have (the name of the vocabulary word she has). Who has the definition?" The round continues until all words and definitions have been given.

Things Fall Apart Word List

No.	Word	Clue/Definition
1.	ACHEBE	Author
2.	AGBALA	Oracle of the Hills and Caves
3.	BICYCLE	The iron horse
4.	BROWN	First missionary in Umuofia: Mr. ___
5.	CHIELO	Priestess of the Oracle
6.	CHRISTIANITY	The white men's faith
7.	CHUKWU	The major god of the villagers
8.	COMMISSIONER	Was writing a book about his experiences in Africa
9.	COWRIES	Shells used for money
10.	DESPAIR	What Okonkwo felt when he began his exile
11.	EGWUGWU	Masqueraders who impersonate ancestral spirits
12.	EKWEFI	Okonkwo's second wife and mother of Ezinma
13.	ENOCH	Unmasked an egwugwu
14.	EXILE	Okonkwo's punishment for accidentally shooting the boy
15.	EZEUDU	Clan elder who had tumultuous funeral
16.	FATHER	What Ikemefuna called Okonkwo
17.	FOREST	Where the Christians built their church; Evil ___
18.	GOVERNMENT	What the white man brought in addition to religion
19.	HANGED	How Okonkwo killed himself
20.	IKEMEFUNA	Murdered by the clan
21.	KIAGA	In charge of the church in Umuofia after the white man left; Mr. ___
22.	KOLA	Nuts offered in hospitality
23.	LEPROSY	Clan translation for
24.	LOCUSTS	Delicacy caught and roasted by villagers
25.	MACHETE	Weapon Okonkwo used to kill the government messenger
26.	MBANTA	Where Okonkwo lived in exile
27.	MISSIONARIES	Came to convert the African natives
28.	NWOYE	Okonkwo's son who converted to Christianity
29.	OBI	Traditional dwelling or hut
30.	OBIERIKA	Okonkwo's friend
31.	OGBANGE	Child who dies and returns to be reborn
32.	OKONKWO	Successful, strong central character of novel
33.	ORACLE	Consulted before decisions were made by the clan
34.	PALM	Type of wine the villagers drank
35.	PRISON	Where Okonkwo and the others went for destroying the church
36.	PYTHON	Sacred animal
37.	RELIGION	What white men brought, along with government
38.	SEVEN	Number of years of Okonkwo's exile
39.	SMITH	Mr. Brown's unpleasant successor; Mr. ___
40.	SUPREME	What Mother is, according to Uchendu
41.	UCHENDU	Welcomed Okonkwo in Mbanta
42.	UMUOFIA	Okonkwo's home
43.	UNOKA	Okonkwo's unsuccessful father
44.	WRESTLING	How Okonkwo won his early fame
45.	YAMS	Major food crop

Things Fall Apart Fill In The Blank 1

_____

1. What the white man brought in addition to religion
2. Was writing a book about his experiences in Africa
3. How Okonkwo won his early fame
4. Clan translation for
5. Came to convert the African natives
6. Welcomed Okonkwo in Mbanta
7. Sacred animal
8. Okonkwo's punishment for accidentally shooting the boy
9. Where the Christians built their church; Evil ___
10. Number of years of Okonkwo's exile
11. Okonkwo's unsuccessful father
12. Priestess of the Oracle
13. Okonkwo's home
14. Major food crop
15. Okonkwo's son who converted to Christianity
16. Weapon Okonkwo used to kill the government messenger
17. Okonkwo's friend
18. Clan elder who had tumultuous funeral
19. Shells used for money
20. Mr. Brown's unpleasant successor; Mr. ___

Things Fall Apart Fill In The Blank 1 Answer Key

GOVERNMENT	1. What the white man brought in addition to religion
COMMISSIONER	2. Was writing a book about his experiences in Africa
WRESTLING	3. How Okonkwo won his early fame
LEPROSY	4. Clan translation for
MISSIONARIES	5. Came to convert the African natives
UCHENDU	6. Welcomed Okonkwo in Mbanta
PYTHON	7. Sacred animal
EXILE	8. Okonkwo's punishment for accidentally shooting the boy
FOREST	9. Where the Christians built their church; Evil ___
SEVEN	10. Number of years of Okonkwo's exile
UNOKA	11. Okonkwo's unsuccessful father
CHIELO	12. Priestess of the Oracle
UMUOFIA	13. Okonkwo's home
YAMS	14. Major food crop
NWOYE	15. Okonkwo's son who converted to Christianity
MACHETE	16. Weapon Okonkwo used to kill the government messenger
OBIERIKA	17. Okonkwo's friend
EZEUDU	18. Clan elder who had tumultuous funeral
COWRIES	19. Shells used for money
SMITH	20. Mr. Brown's unpleasant successor; Mr. ___

Things Fall Apart Fill In The Blank 2

_____

_____

_____

_____

_____

_____

_____

_____

_____

_____

_____

_____

_____

_____

_____

_____

_____

_____

_____

_____

1. Successful, strong central character of novel
2. Okonkwo's son who converted to Christianity
3. Nuts offered in hospitality
4. What Mother is, according to Uchendu
5. Mr. Brown's unpleasant successor; Mr. ___
6. Clan elder who had tumultuous funeral
7. Murdered by the clan
8. Unmasked an egwugwu
9. First missionary in Umuofia: Mr. ___
10. Okonkwo's friend
11. Sacred animal
12. Was writing a book about his experiences in Africa
13. Priestess of the Oracle
14. In charge of the church in Umuofia after the white man left; Mr. ___
15. The major god of the villagers
16. The white men's faith
17. Number of years of Okonkwo's exile
18. Consulted before decisions were made by the clan
19. Clan translation for
20. Shells used for money

Things Fall Apart Fill In The Blank 2 Answer Key

OKONKWO	1. Successful, strong central character of novel
NWOYE	2. Okonkwo's son who converted to Christianity
KOLA	3. Nuts offered in hospitality
SUPREME	4. What Mother is, according to Uchendu
SMITH	5. Mr. Brown's unpleasant successor; Mr. ___
EZEUDU	6. Clan elder who had tumultuous funeral
IKEMEFUNA	7. Murdered by the clan
ENOCH	8. Unmasked an egwugwu
BROWN	9. First missionary in Umuofia: Mr. ___
OBIERIKA	10. Okonkwo's friend
PYTHON	11. Sacred animal
COMMISSIONER	12. Was writing a book about his experiences in Africa
CHIELO	13. Priestess of the Oracle
KIAGA	14. In charge of the church in Umuofia after the white man left; Mr. ___
CHUKWU	15. The major god of the villagers
CHRISTIANITY	16. The white men's faith
SEVEN	17. Number of years of Okonkwo's exile
ORACLE	18. Consulted before decisions were made by the clan
LEPROSY	19. Clan translation for
COWRIES	20. Shells used for money

Things Fall Apart Fill In The Blank 3

_____ 1. Okonkwo's punishment for accidentally shooting the boy
_____ 2. What Mother is, according to Uchendu
_____ 3. Child who dies and returns to be reborn
_____ 4. What white men brought, along with government
_____ 5. Okonkwo's friend
_____ 6. Weapon Okonkwo used to kill the government messenger
_____ 7. Okonkwo's son who converted to Christianity
_____ 8. Murdered by the clan
_____ 9. Priestess of the Oracle
_____ 10. Author
_____ 11. In charge of the church in Umuofia after the white man left; Mr. ___
_____ 12. Okonkwo's home
_____ 13. Unmasked an egwugwu
_____ 14. What the white man brought in addition to religion
_____ 15. Where Okonkwo lived in exile
_____ 16. How Okonkwo won his early fame
_____ 17. Okonkwo's unsuccessful father
_____ 18. Number of years of Okonkwo's exile
_____ 19. Came to convert the African natives
_____ 20. Sacred animal

Things Fall Apart Fill In The Blank 3 Answer Key

EXILE	1. Okonkwo's punishment for accidentally shooting the boy
SUPREME	2. What Mother is, according to Uchendu
OGBANGE	3. Child who dies and returns to be reborn
RELIGION	4. What white men brought, along with government
OBIERIKA	5. Okonkwo's friend
MACHETE	6. Weapon Okonkwo used to kill the government messenger
NWOYE	7. Okonkwo's son who converted to Christianity
IKEMEFUNA	8. Murdered by the clan
CHIELO	9. Priestess of the Oracle
ACHEBE	10. Author
KIAGA	11. In charge of the church in Umuofia after the white man left; Mr. ___
UMUOFIA	12. Okonkwo's home
ENOCH	13. Unmasked an egwugwu
GOVERNMENT	14. What the white man brought in addition to religion
MBANTA	15. Where Okonkwo lived in exile
WRESTLING	16. How Okonkwo won his early fame
UNOKA	17. Okonkwo's unsuccessful father
SEVEN	18. Number of years of Okonkwo's exile
MISSIONARIES	19. Came to convert the African natives
PYTHON	20. Sacred animal

Things Fall Apart Fill In The Blank 4

_____

_____

_____

_____

_____

_____

_____

_____

_____

_____

_____

_____

_____

_____

_____

_____

_____

_____

_____

_____

1. Where the Christians built their church; Evil ___
2. Oracle of the Hills and Caves
3. Where Okonkwo and the others went for destroying the church
4. What Okonkwo felt when he began his exile
5. Okonkwo's second wife and mother of Ezinma
6. What Ikemefuna called Okonkwo
7. Murdered by the clan
8. The white men's faith
9. What the white man brought in addition to religion
10. The iron horse
11. What Mother is, according to Uchendu
12. Masqueraders who impersonate ancestral spirits
13. How Okonkwo won his early fame
14. The major god of the villagers
15. Clan elder who had tumultuous funeral
16. In charge of the church in Umuofia after the white man left; Mr. ___
17. Okonkwo's home
18. Priestess of the Oracle
19. Successful, strong central character of novel
20. First missionary in Umuofia: Mr. ___

Things Fall Apart Fill In The Blank 4 Answer Key

Answer	#	Clue
FOREST	1.	Where the Christians built their church; Evil ___
AGBALA	2.	Oracle of the Hills and Caves
PRISON	3.	Where Okonkwo and the others went for destroying the church
DESPAIR	4.	What Okonkwo felt when he began his exile
EKWEFI	5.	Okonkwo's second wife and mother of Ezinma
FATHER	6.	What Ikemefuna called Okonkwo
IKEMEFUNA	7.	Murdered by the clan
CHRISTIANITY	8.	The white men's faith
GOVERNMENT	9.	What the white man brought in addition to religion
BICYCLE	10.	The iron horse
SUPREME	11.	What Mother is, according to Uchendu
EGWUGWU	12.	Masqueraders who impersonate ancestral spirits
WRESTLING	13.	How Okonkwo won his early fame
CHUKWU	14.	The major god of the villagers
EZEUDU	15.	Clan elder who had tumultuous funeral
KIAGA	16.	In charge of the church in Umuofia after the white man left; Mr. ___
UMUOFIA	17.	Okonkwo's home
CHIELO	18.	Priestess of the Oracle
OKONKWO	19.	Successful, strong central character of novel
BROWN	20.	First missionary in Umuofia: Mr. ___

Things Fall Apart Matching 1

___ 1. KOLA	A. Nuts offered in hospitality
___ 2. ACHEBE	B. In charge of the church in Umuofia after the white man left; Mr. ___
___ 3. ORACLE	C. Shells used for money
___ 4. LOCUSTS	D. Number of years of Okonkwo's exile
___ 5. NWOYE	E. Where the Christians built their church; Evil ___
___ 6. COWRIES	F. Child who dies and returns to be reborn
___ 7. SUPREME	G. Author
___ 8. SEVEN	H. Welcomed Okonkwo in Mbanta
___ 9. KIAGA	I. Traditional dwelling or hut
___ 10. BICYCLE	J. The major god of the villagers
___ 11. LEPROSY	K. How Okonkwo killed himself
___ 12. HANGED	L. Where Okonkwo lived in exile
___ 13. CHUKWU	M. Okonkwo's son who converted to Christianity
___ 14. UCHENDU	N. Came to convert the African natives
___ 15. PALM	O. Murdered by the clan
___ 16. FOREST	P. What Mother is, according to Uchendu
___ 17. MBANTA	Q. Oracle of the Hills and Caves
___ 18. IKEMEFUNA	R. The iron horse
___ 19. MISSIONARIES	S. What Ikemefuna called Okonkwo
___ 20. CHRISTIANITY	T. The white men's faith
___ 21. OBI	U. Consulted before decisions were made by the clan
___ 22. YAMS	V. Type of wine the villagers drank
___ 23. AGBALA	W. Major food crop
___ 24. FATHER	X. Clan translation for
___ 25. OGBANGE	Y. Delicacy caught and roasted by villagers

Things Fall Apart Matching 1 Answer Key

A - 1. KOLA	A.	Nuts offered in hospitality
G - 2. ACHEBE	B.	In charge of the church in Umuofia after the white man left; Mr. ___
U - 3. ORACLE	C.	Shells used for money
Y - 4. LOCUSTS	D.	Number of years of Okonkwo's exile
M - 5. NWOYE	E.	Where the Christians built their church; Evil ___
C - 6. COWRIES	F.	Child who dies and returns to be reborn
P - 7. SUPREME	G.	Author
D - 8. SEVEN	H.	Welcomed Okonkwo in Mbanta
B - 9. KIAGA	I.	Traditional dwelling or hut
R - 10. BICYCLE	J.	The major god of the villagers
X - 11. LEPROSY	K.	How Okonkwo killed himself
K - 12. HANGED	L.	Where Okonkwo lived in exile
J - 13. CHUKWU	M.	Okonkwo's son who converted to Christianity
H - 14. UCHENDU	N.	Came to convert the African natives
V - 15. PALM	O.	Murdered by the clan
E - 16. FOREST	P.	What Mother is, according to Uchendu
L - 17. MBANTA	Q.	Oracle of the Hills and Caves
O - 18. IKEMEFUNA	R.	The iron horse
N - 19. MISSIONARIES	S.	What Ikemefuna called Okonkwo
T - 20. CHRISTIANITY	T.	The white men's faith
I - 21. OBI	U.	Consulted before decisions were made by the clan
W - 22. YAMS	V.	Type of wine the villagers drank
Q - 23. AGBALA	W.	Major food crop
S - 24. FATHER	X.	Clan translation for
F - 25. OGBANGE	Y.	Delicacy caught and roasted by villagers

Things Fall Apart Matching 2

___ 1. MISSIONARIES   A. Came to convert the African natives
___ 2. EXILE   B. Type of wine the villagers drank
___ 3. NWOYE   C. Shells used for money
___ 4. SMITH   D. Delicacy caught and roasted by villagers
___ 5. CHRISTIANITY   E. Okonkwo's home
___ 6. YAMS   F. Oracle of the Hills and Caves
___ 7. LOCUSTS   G. Okonkwo's punishment for accidentally shooting the boy
___ 8. GOVERNMENT   H. What white men brought, along with government
___ 9. PYTHON   I. What the white man brought in addition to religion
___10. ORACLE   J. Mr. Brown's unpleasant successor; Mr. ___
___11. PRISON   K. Nuts offered in hospitality
___12. RELIGION   L. Okonkwo's friend
___13. HANGED   M. Traditional dwelling or hut
___14. UMUOFIA   N. Sacred animal
___15. AGBALA   O. Where Okonkwo and the others went for destroying the church
___16. PALM   P. The white men's faith
___17. KOLA   Q. Consulted before decisions were made by the clan
___18. EKWEFI   R. What Mother is, according to Uchendu
___19. OBI   S. The major god of the villagers
___20. CHUKWU   T. How Okonkwo killed himself
___21. OBIERIKA   U. Unmasked an egwugwu
___22. COWRIES   V. Okonkwo's second wife and mother of Ezinma
___23. ENOCH   W. Major food crop
___24. UCHENDU   X. Welcomed Okonkwo in Mbanta
___25. SUPREME   Y. Okonkwo's son who converted to Christianity

Things Fall Apart Matching 2 Answer Key

A - 1. MISSIONARIES		A. Came to convert the African natives
G - 2. EXILE		B. Type of wine the villagers drank
Y - 3. NWOYE		C. Shells used for money
J - 4. SMITH		D. Delicacy caught and roasted by villagers
P - 5. CHRISTIANITY		E. Okonkwo's home
W - 6. YAMS		F. Oracle of the Hills and Caves
D - 7. LOCUSTS		G. Okonkwo's punishment for accidentally shooting the boy
I - 8. GOVERNMENT		H. What white men brought, along with government
N - 9. PYTHON		I. What the white man brought in addition to religion
Q - 10. ORACLE		J. Mr. Brown's unpleasant successor; Mr. ___
O - 11. PRISON		K. Nuts offered in hospitality
H - 12. RELIGION		L. Okonkwo's friend
T - 13. HANGED		M. Traditional dwelling or hut
E - 14. UMUOFIA		N. Sacred animal
F - 15. AGBALA		O. Where Okonkwo and the others went for destroying the church
B - 16. PALM		P. The white men's faith
K - 17. KOLA		Q. Consulted before decisions were made by the clan
V - 18. EKWEFI		R. What Mother is, according to Uchendu
M - 19. OBI		S. The major god of the villagers
S - 20. CHUKWU		T. How Okonkwo killed himself
L - 21. OBIERIKA		U. Unmasked an egwugwu
C - 22. COWRIES		V. Okonkwo's second wife and mother of Ezinma
U - 23. ENOCH		W. Major food crop
X - 24. UCHENDU		X. Welcomed Okonkwo in Mbanta
R - 25. SUPREME		Y. Okonkwo's son who converted to Christianity

Things Fall Apart Matching 3

___ 1. UCHENDU   A. Okonkwo's son who converted to Christianity
___ 2. IKEMEFUNA   B. The iron horse
___ 3. ENOCH   C. Okonkwo's second wife and mother of Ezinma
___ 4. EKWEFI   D. Murdered by the clan
___ 5. MBANTA   E. Was writing a book about his experiences in Africa
___ 6. SEVEN   F. Unmasked an egwugwu
___ 7. GOVERNMENT   G. Number of years of Okonkwo's exile
___ 8. OKONKWO   H. What the white man brought in addition to religion
___ 9. EXILE   I. Delicacy caught and roasted by villagers
___ 10. EZEUDU   J. Okonkwo's punishment for accidentally shooting the boy
___ 11. SUPREME   K. Came to convert the African natives
___ 12. KOLA   L. Child who dies and returns to be reborn
___ 13. FOREST   M. Successful, strong central character of novel
___ 14. YAMS   N. How Okonkwo won his early fame
___ 15. FATHER   O. Where Okonkwo lived in exile
___ 16. COMMISSIONER   P. What Mother is, according to Uchendu
___ 17. BICYCLE   Q. Weapon Okonkwo used to kill the government messenger
___ 18. NWOYE   R. Welcomed Okonkwo in Mbanta
___ 19. OBIERIKA   S. Clan elder who had tumultuous funeral
___ 20. LOCUSTS   T. Okonkwo's friend
___ 21. MISSIONARIES   U. Nuts offered in hospitality
___ 22. OGBANGE   V. What Ikemefuna called Okonkwo
___ 23. ACHEBE   W. Major food crop
___ 24. MACHETE   X. Where the Christians built their church; Evil ___
___ 25. WRESTLING   Y. Author

Things Fall Apart Matching 3 Answer Key

R - 1. UCHENDU	A. Okonkwo's son who converted to Christianity
D - 2. IKEMEFUNA	B. The iron horse
F - 3. ENOCH	C. Okonkwo's second wife and mother of Ezinma
C - 4. EKWEFI	D. Murdered by the clan
O - 5. MBANTA	E. Was writing a book about his experiences in Africa
G - 6. SEVEN	F. Unmasked an egwugwu
H - 7. GOVERNMENT	G. Number of years of Okonkwo's exile
M - 8. OKONKWO	H. What the white man brought in addition to religion
J - 9. EXILE	I. Delicacy caught and roasted by villagers
S - 10. EZEUDU	J. Okonkwo's punishment for accidentally shooting the boy
P - 11. SUPREME	K. Came to convert the African natives
U - 12. KOLA	L. Child who dies and returns to be reborn
X - 13. FOREST	M. Successful, strong central character of novel
W - 14. YAMS	N. How Okonkwo won his early fame
V - 15. FATHER	O. Where Okonkwo lived in exile
E - 16. COMMISSIONER	P. What Mother is, according to Uchendu
B - 17. BICYCLE	Q. Weapon Okonkwo used to kill the government messenger
A - 18. NWOYE	R. Welcomed Okonkwo in Mbanta
T - 19. OBIERIKA	S. Clan elder who had tumultuous funeral
I - 20. LOCUSTS	T. Okonkwo's friend
K - 21. MISSIONARIES	U. Nuts offered in hospitality
L - 22. OGBANGE	V. What Ikemefuna called Okonkwo
Y - 23. ACHEBE	W. Major food crop
Q - 24. MACHETE	X. Where the Christians built their church; Evil ___
N - 25. WRESTLING	Y. Author

Things Fall Apart Matching 4

___ 1. LEPROSY
___ 2. UMUOFIA
___ 3. FOREST
___ 4. EZEUDU
___ 5. UCHENDU
___ 6. SEVEN
___ 7. PRISON
___ 8. ACHEBE
___ 9. ENOCH
___ 10. LOCUSTS
___ 11. AGBALA
___ 12. OBI
___ 13. HANGED
___ 14. MBANTA
___ 15. OGBANGE
___ 16. WRESTLING
___ 17. PYTHON
___ 18. COWRIES
___ 19. BICYCLE
___ 20. YAMS
___ 21. SUPREME
___ 22. PALM
___ 23. RELIGION
___ 24. EXILE
___ 25. KIAGA

A. Delicacy caught and roasted by villagers
B. Okonkwo's punishment for accidentally shooting the boy
C. Where Okonkwo and the others went for destroying the church
D. Welcomed Okonkwo in Mbanta
E. Child who dies and returns to be reborn
F. Where the Christians built their church; Evil ___
G. Shells used for money
H. Major food crop
I. Traditional dwelling or hut
J. How Okonkwo killed himself
K. Clan translation for
L. Okonkwo's home
M. Clan elder who had tumultuous funeral
N. Where Okonkwo lived in exile
O. The iron horse
P. In charge of the church in Umuofia after the white man left; Mr. ___
Q. Author
R. Number of years of Okonkwo's exile
S. Type of wine the villagers drank
T. Unmasked an egwugwu
U. Oracle of the Hills and Caves
V. What white men brought, along with government
W. What Mother is, according to Uchendu
X. How Okonkwo won his early fame
Y. Sacred animal

Things Fall Apart Matching 4 Answer Key

K - 1. LEPROSY	A. Delicacy caught and roasted by villagers
L - 2. UMUOFIA	B. Okonkwo's punishment for accidentally shooting the boy
F - 3. FOREST	C. Where Okonkwo and the others went for destroying the church
M - 4. EZEUDU	D. Welcomed Okonkwo in Mbanta
D - 5. UCHENDU	E. Child who dies and returns to be reborn
R - 6. SEVEN	F. Where the Christians built their church; Evil ___
C - 7. PRISON	G. Shells used for money
Q - 8. ACHEBE	H. Major food crop
T - 9. ENOCH	I. Traditional dwelling or hut
A - 10. LOCUSTS	J. How Okonkwo killed himself
U - 11. AGBALA	K. Clan translation for
I - 12. OBI	L. Okonkwo's home
J - 13. HANGED	M. Clan elder who had tumultuous funeral
N - 14. MBANTA	N. Where Okonkwo lived in exile
E - 15. OGBANGE	O. The iron horse
X - 16. WRESTLING	P. In charge of the church in Umuofia after the white man left; Mr. ___
Y - 17. PYTHON	Q. Author
G - 18. COWRIES	R. Number of years of Okonkwo's exile
O - 19. BICYCLE	S. Type of wine the villagers drank
H - 20. YAMS	T. Unmasked an egwugwu
W - 21. SUPREME	U. Oracle of the Hills and Caves
S - 22. PALM	V. What white men brought, along with government
V - 23. RELIGION	W. What Mother is, according to Uchendu
B - 24. EXILE	X. How Okonkwo won his early fame
P - 25. KIAGA	Y. Sacred animal

Things Fall Apart Magic Squares 1

Match the definition with the vocabulary word. Put your answers in the magic squares below. When your answers are correct, all columns and rows will add to the same number.

A. ENOCH
B. KOLA
C. EXILE
D. COMMISSIONER
E. SEVEN
F. AGBALA
G. CHUKWU
H. FOREST
I. LOCUSTS
J. SUPREME
K. DESPAIR
L. UNOKA
M. UMUOFIA
N. RELIGION
O. COWRIES
P. OGBANGE

1. Nuts offered in hospitality
2. The major god of the villagers
3. What Okonkwo felt when he began his exile
4. What white men brought, along with government
5. Okonkwo's home
6. Okonkwo's unsuccessful father
7. Where the Christians built their church; Evil ___
8. Unmasked an egwugwu
9. Child who dies and returns to be reborn
10. Delicacy caught and roasted by villagers
11. Number of years of Okonkwo's exile
12. Was writing a book about his experiences in Africa
13. Okonkwo's punishment for accidentally shooting the boy
14. Oracle of the Hills and Caves
15. What Mother is, according to Uchendu
16. Shells used for money

A=	B=	C=	D=
E=	F=	G=	H=
I=	J=	K=	L=
M=	N=	O=	P=

Things Fall Apart Magic Squares 1 Answer Key

Match the definition with the vocabulary word. Put your answers in the magic squares below. When your answers are correct, all columns and rows will add to the same number.

A. ENOCH
B. KOLA
C. EXILE
D. COMMISSIONER
E. SEVEN
F. AGBALA

G. CHUKWU
H. FOREST
I. LOCUSTS
J. SUPREME
K. DESPAIR
L. UNOKA

M. UMUOFIA
N. RELIGION
O. COWRIES
P. OGBANGE

1. Nuts offered in hospitality
2. The major god of the villagers
3. What Okonkwo felt when he began his exile
4. What white men brought, along with government
5. Okonkwo's home
6. Okonkwo's unsuccessful father
7. Where the Christians built their church; Evil ___
8. Unmasked an egwugwu
9. Child who dies and returns to be reborn
10. Delicacy caught and roasted by villagers
11. Number of years of Okonkwo's exile
12. Was writing a book about his experiences in Africa
13. Okonkwo's punishment for accidentally shooting the boy
14. Oracle of the Hills and Caves
15. What Mother is, according to Uchendu
16. Shells used for money

A=8	B=1	C=13	D=12
E=11	F=14	G=2	H=7
I=10	J=15	K=3	L=6
M=5	N=4	O=16	P=9

Things Fall Apart Magic Squares 2

Match the definition with the vocabulary word. Put your answers in the magic squares below. When your answers are correct, all columns and rows will add to the same number.

A. CHRISTIANITY
B. MACHETE
C. BICYCLE
D. OBI
E. GOVERNMENT
F. SMITH
G. CHIELO
H. OGBANGE
I. PALM
J. RELIGION
K. NWOYE
L. UCHENDU
M. FOREST
N. MBANTA
O. FATHER
P. KOLA

1. The iron horse
2. What white men brought, along with government
3. Mr. Brown's unpleasant successor; Mr. ___
4. What Ikemefuna called Okonkwo
5. Nuts offered in hospitality
6. What the white man brought in addition to religion
7. Type of wine the villagers drank
8. Traditional dwelling or hut
9. Where the Christians built their church; Evil ___
10. Child who dies and returns to be reborn
11. Welcomed Okonkwo in Mbanta
12. The white men's faith
13. Weapon Okonkwo used to kill the government messenger
14. Okonkwo's son who converted to Christianity
15. Priestess of the Oracle
16. Where Okonkwo lived in exile

A=	B=	C=	D=
E=	F=	G=	H=
I=	J=	K=	L=
M=	N=	O=	P=

Things Fall Apart Magic Squares 2 Answer Key

Match the definition with the vocabulary word. Put your answers in the magic squares below. When your answers are correct, all columns and rows will add to the same number.

A. CHRISTIANITY
B. MACHETE
C. BICYCLE
D. OBI
E. GOVERNMENT
F. SMITH

G. CHIELO
H. OGBANGE
I. PALM
J. RELIGION
K. NWOYE
L. UCHENDU

M. FOREST
N. MBANTA
O. FATHER
P. KOLA

1. The iron horse
2. What white men brought, along with government
3. Mr. Brown's unpleasant successor; Mr. ___
4. What Ikemefuna called Okonkwo
5. Nuts offered in hospitality
6. What the white man brought in addition to religion
7. Type of wine the villagers drank
8. Traditional dwelling or hut
9. Where the Christians built their church; Evil ___
10. Child who dies and returns to be reborn
11. Welcomed Okonkwo in Mbanta
12. The white men's faith
13. Weapon Okonkwo used to kill the government messenger
14. Okonkwo's son who converted to Christianity
15. Priestess of the Oracle
16. Where Okonkwo lived in exile

A=12	B=13	C=1	D=8
E=6	F=3	G=15	H=10
I=7	J=2	K=14	L=11
M=9	N=16	O=4	P=5

Things Fall Apart Magic Squares 3

Match the definition with the vocabulary word. Put your answers in the magic squares below. When your answers are correct, all columns and rows will add to the same number.

A. YAMS
B. LEPROSY
C. PRISON
D. OBIERIKA
E. SUPREME
F. MACHETE
G. OKONKWO
H. SMITH
I. KOLA
J. PALM
K. EZEUDU
L. GOVERNMENT
M. LOCUSTS
N. KIAGA
O. MISSIONARIES
P. EKWEFI

1. Weapon Okonkwo used to kill the government messenger
2. Nuts offered in hospitality
3. Came to convert the African natives
4. Okonkwo's friend
5. Delicacy caught and roasted by villagers
6. Clan translation for
7. Mr. Brown's unpleasant successor; Mr. ___
8. Clan elder who had tumultuous funeral
9. Where Okonkwo and the others went for destroying the church
10. Okonkwo's second wife and mother of Ezinma
11. Type of wine the villagers drank
12. What Mother is, according to Uchendu
13. What the white man brought in addition to religion
14. Successful, strong central character of novel
15. Major food crop
16. In charge of the church in Umuofia after the white man left; Mr. ___

A=	B=	C=	D=
E=	F=	G=	H=
I=	J=	K=	L=
M=	N=	O=	P=

Things Fall Apart Magic Squares 3 Answer Key

Match the definition with the vocabulary word. Put your answers in the magic squares below. When your answers are correct, all columns and rows will add to the same number.

A. YAMS
B. LEPROSY
C. PRISON
D. OBIERIKA
E. SUPREME
F. MACHETE
G. OKONKWO
H. SMITH
I. KOLA
J. PALM
K. EZEUDU
L. GOVERNMENT
M. LOCUSTS
N. KIAGA
O. MISSIONARIES
P. EKWEFI

1. Weapon Okonkwo used to kill the government messenger
2. Nuts offered in hospitality
3. Came to convert the African natives
4. Okonkwo's friend
5. Delicacy caught and roasted by villagers
6. Clan translation for
7. Mr. Brown's unpleasant successor; Mr. ___
8. Clan elder who had tumultuous funeral
9. Where Okonkwo and the others went for destroying the church
10. Okonkwo's second wife and mother of Ezinma
11. Type of wine the villagers drank
12. What Mother is, according to Uchendu
13. What the white man brought in addition to religion
14. Successful, strong central character of novel
15. Major food crop
16. In charge of the church in Umuofia after the white man left; Mr. ___

A=15	B=6	C=9	D=4
E=12	F=1	G=14	H=7
I=2	J=11	K=8	L=13
M=5	N=16	O=3	P=10

Things Fall Apart Magic Squares 4

Match the definition with the vocabulary word. Put your answers in the magic squares below. When your answers are correct, all columns and rows will add to the same number.

A. MBANTA
B. ORACLE
C. YAMS
D. PRISON
E. BICYCLE
F. FOREST
G. BROWN
H. OBIERIKA
I. UCHENDU
J. MISSIONARIES
K. PYTHON
L. LOCUSTS
M. HANGED
N. IKEMEFUNA
O. EKWEFI
P. UNOKA

1. Okonkwo's friend
2. How Okonkwo killed himself
3. Consulted before decisions were made by the clan
4. Sacred animal
5. Came to convert the African natives
6. Major food crop
7. Okonkwo's unsuccessful father
8. The iron horse
9. Okonkwo's second wife and mother of Ezinma
10. Where the Christians built their church; Evil ___
11. Welcomed Okonkwo in Mbanta
12. Where Okonkwo and the others went for destroying the church
13. Where Okonkwo lived in exile
14. Delicacy caught and roasted by villagers
15. First missionary in Umuofia: Mr. ___
16. Murdered by the clan

A=	B=	C=	D=
E=	F=	G=	H=
I=	J=	K=	L=
M=	N=	O=	P=

Things Fall Apart Magic Squares 4 Answer Key

Match the definition with the vocabulary word. Put your answers in the magic squares below. When your answers are correct, all columns and rows will add to the same number.

A. MBANTA
B. ORACLE
C. YAMS
D. PRISON
E. BICYCLE
F. FOREST
G. BROWN
H. OBIERIKA
I. UCHENDU
J. MISSIONARIES
K. PYTHON
L. LOCUSTS
M. HANGED
N. IKEMEFUNA
O. EKWEFI
P. UNOKA

1. Okonkwo's friend
2. How Okonkwo killed himself
3. Consulted before decisions were made by the clan
4. Sacred animal
5. Came to convert the African natives
6. Major food crop
7. Okonkwo's unsuccessful father
8. The iron horse
9. Okonkwo's second wife and mother of Ezinma
10. Where the Christians built their church; Evil ___
11. Welcomed Okonkwo in Mbanta
12. Where Okonkwo and the others went for destroying the church
13. Where Okonkwo lived in exile
14. Delicacy caught and roasted by villagers
15. First missionary in Umuofia: Mr. ___
16. Murdered by the clan

A=13	B=3	C=6	D=12
A=8	F=10	G=15	H=1
I=11	J=5	K=4	L=14
M=2	N=16	O=9	P=7

Things Fall Apart Word Search 1

Words are placed backwards, forward, diagonally, up and down. Clues listed below can help you find the words. Circle the hidden vocabulary words in the maze.

```
C H R I S T I A N I T Y O R A C L E
L Y W C U A S Q Z B D N F O R E S T
J Z M O C G E C H I E L O W L C G H
P M A W H B I D W L S W R C D H V H
H P C R E A R L V T P P Y E R U K Q
F R H I N L A G N R A C M N E K I T
Z A E E D A N W E L I E E K A W A D
P S T S U C O L M B R O W N U G F
R Y E H F Y I W C P K E U W O N A Q
I U T B E G S D U L F F G M I C H V
S N M H I R S S U I E U S L M E H E
O O C O O M I X H M W P T M L Y G J
N K N S A N M F E G U S R I I N F A
W A D Y S P D K E K E O X O A T T Q
H A N G E D I O W R K E F B S N H Z
F X N H V W H B W X S O G I A Y Q H
D A C H E B E I S C S O L B A S Y J
R S S Q N E Z E U D U C M A R M M T
```

Clan translation for (7)
Author (6)
Came to convert the African natives (12)
Child who dies and returns to be reborn (7)
Clan elder who had tumultuous funeral (6)
Consulted before decisions were made by the clan (6)
Delicacy caught and roasted by villagers (7)
First missionary in Umuofia: Mr. ___ (5)
How Okonkwo killed himself (6)
How Okonkwo won his early fame (9)
In charge of the church in Umuofia after the white man left; Mr. ___ (5)
Major food crop (4)
Masqueraders who impersonate ancestral spirits (7)
Mr. Brown's unpleasant successor; Mr. ___ (5)
Murdered by the clan (9)
Number of years of Okonkwo's exile (5)
Nuts offered in hospitality (4)
Okonkwo's home (7)
Okonkwo's punishment for accidentally shooting the boy (5)
Okonkwo's second wife and mother of Ezinma (6)
Okonkwo's son who converted to Christianity (5)
Okonkwo's unsuccessful father (5)
Oracle of the Hills and Caves (6)
Priestess of the Oracle (6)
Sacred animal (6)
Shells used for money (7)
The iron horse (7)
The major god of the villagers (6)
The white men's faith (12)
Traditional dwelling or hut (3)
Type of wine the villagers drank (4)
Unmasked an egwugwu (5)
Weapon Okonkwo used to kill the government messenger (7)
Welcomed Okonkwo in Mbanta (7)
What Ikemefuna called Okonkwo (6)
What Mother is, according to Uchendu (7)
What Okonkwo felt when he began his exile (7)
What white men brought, along with government (8)
Where Okonkwo and the others went for destroying the church (6)
Where Okonkwo lived in exile (6)
Where the Christians built their church; Evil ___ (6)

Things Fall Apart Word Search 1 Answer Key

Words are placed backwards, forward, diagonally, up and down. Clues listed below can help you find the words. Circle the hidden vocabulary words in the maze.

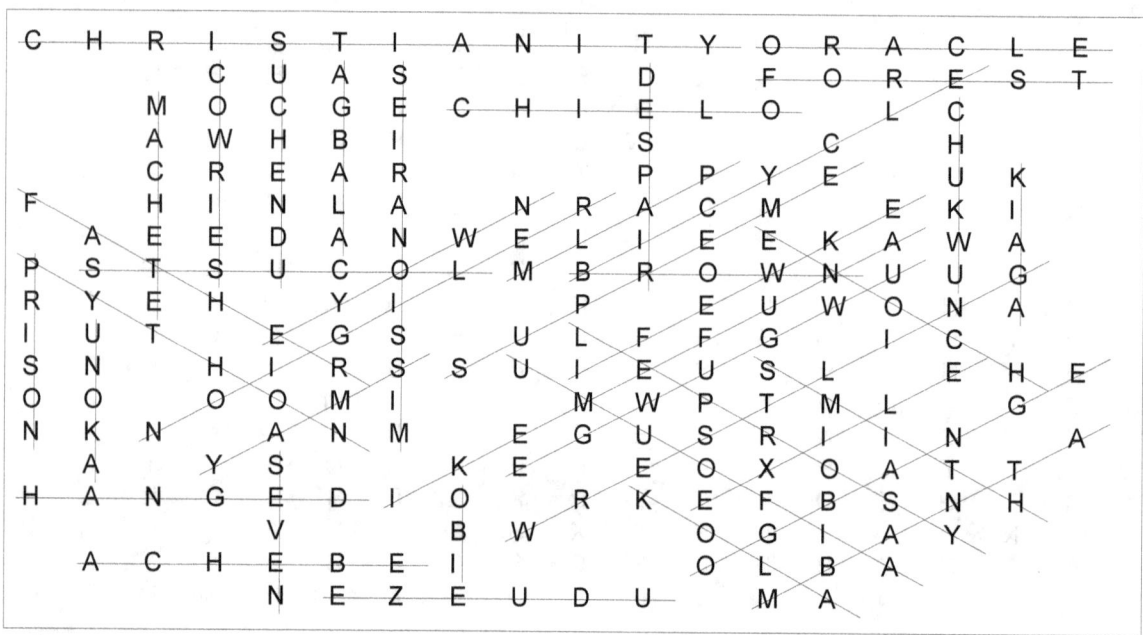

Clan translation for (7)
Author (6)
Came to convert the African natives (12)
Child who dies and returns to be reborn (7)
Clan elder who had tumultuous funeral (6)
Consulted before decisions were made by the clan (6)
Delicacy caught and roasted by villagers (7)
First missionary in Umuofia: Mr. ___ (5)
How Okonkwo killed himself (6)
How Okonkwo won his early fame (9)
In charge of the church in Umuofia after the white man left; Mr. ___ (5)
Major food crop (4)
Masqueraders who impersonate ancestral spirits (7)
Mr. Brown's unpleasant successor; Mr. ___ (5)
Murdered by the clan (9)
Number of years of Okonkwo's exile (5)
Nuts offered in hospitality (4)
Okonkwo's home (7)
Okonkwo's punishment for accidentally shooting the boy (5)
Okonkwo's second wife and mother of Ezinma (6)
Okonkwo's son who converted to Christianity (5)
Okonkwo's unsuccessful father (5)
Oracle of the Hills and Caves (6)
Priestess of the Oracle (6)
Sacred animal (6)
Shells used for money (7)
The iron horse (7)
The major god of the villagers (6)
The white men's faith (12)
Traditional dwelling or hut (3)
Type of wine the villagers drank (4)
Unmasked an egwugwu (5)
Weapon Okonkwo used to kill the government messenger (7)
Welcomed Okonkwo in Mbanta (7)
What Ikemefuna called Okonkwo (6)
What Mother is, according to Uchendu (7)
What Okonkwo felt when he began his exile (7)
What white men brought, along with government (8)
Where Okonkwo and the others went for destroying the church (6)
Where Okonkwo lived in exile (6)
Where the Christians built their church; Evil ___ (6)

Things Fall Apart Word Search 2

Words are placed backwards, forward, diagonally, up and down. Clues listed below can help you find the words. Circle the hidden vocabulary words in the maze.

```
A G B A L A S U W G U W G E C S P G
K E F Q Z M D L O H M V L L H E A R
I M N Y A N K E T K U T Q C I V L D
R E Y Y E M R P B R O W N A E E M P
E R C H N Z E R E P F N J R L N S R
I P C O L K L O X J I M K O O E T G
B U R F M W I S I E A F R W I X S D
O S P I J M G Y L K K M D R O K U K
L B X Y S R I F E W G V A K D L C F
M C I X T O O S L E X N Q J O B O J
B M N C K H N Q S F O F X H F L L Y
A W P I Y K O G D I A E T E H C A M
N C A W M C D N S T O S N W D K S P
T G H L K E L S H Q E N W O O Q M N
A J Z E G P I E L R W V E N C T I T
K V I N B M R R O Z R U R V H T J
B B A X G E N F Y O G B A N G E H V
O H R I A P S E D E Z E U D U G J Y
```

Clan translation for (7)
Author (6)
Came to convert the African natives (12)
Child who dies and returns to be reborn (7)
Clan elder who had tumultuous funeral (6)
Consulted before decisions were made by the clan (6)
Delicacy caught and roasted by villagers (7)
First missionary in Umuofia: Mr. ___ (5)
How Okonkwo killed himself (6)
In charge of the church in Umuofia after the white man left; Mr. ___ (5)
Major food crop (4)
Masqueraders who impersonate ancestral spirits (7)
Mr. Brown's unpleasant successor; Mr. ___ (5)
Number of years of Okonkwo's exile (5)
Nuts offered in hospitality (4)
Okonkwo's friend (8)
Okonkwo's home (7)
Okonkwo's punishment for accidentally shooting the boy (5)
Okonkwo's second wife and mother of Ezinma (6)
Okonkwo's son who converted to Christianity (5)

Okonkwo's unsuccessful father (5)
Oracle of the Hills and Caves (6)
Priestess of the Oracle (6)
Sacred animal (6)
Successful, strong central character of novel (7)
The iron horse (7)
Traditional dwelling or hut (3)
Type of wine the villagers drank (4)
Unmasked an egwugwu (5)
Was writing a book about his experiences in Africa (12)
Weapon Okonkwo used to kill the government messenger (7)
Welcomed Okonkwo in Mbanta (7)
What Ikemefuna called Okonkwo (6)
What Mother is, according to Uchendu (7)
What Okonkwo felt when he began his exile (7)
What white men brought, along with government (8)
Where Okonkwo and the others went for destroying the church (6)
Where Okonkwo lived in exile (6)
Where the Christians built their church; Evil ___ (6)

Things Fall Apart Word Search 2 Answer Key

Words are placed backwards, forward, diagonally, up and down. Clues listed below can help you find the words. Circle the hidden vocabulary words in the maze.

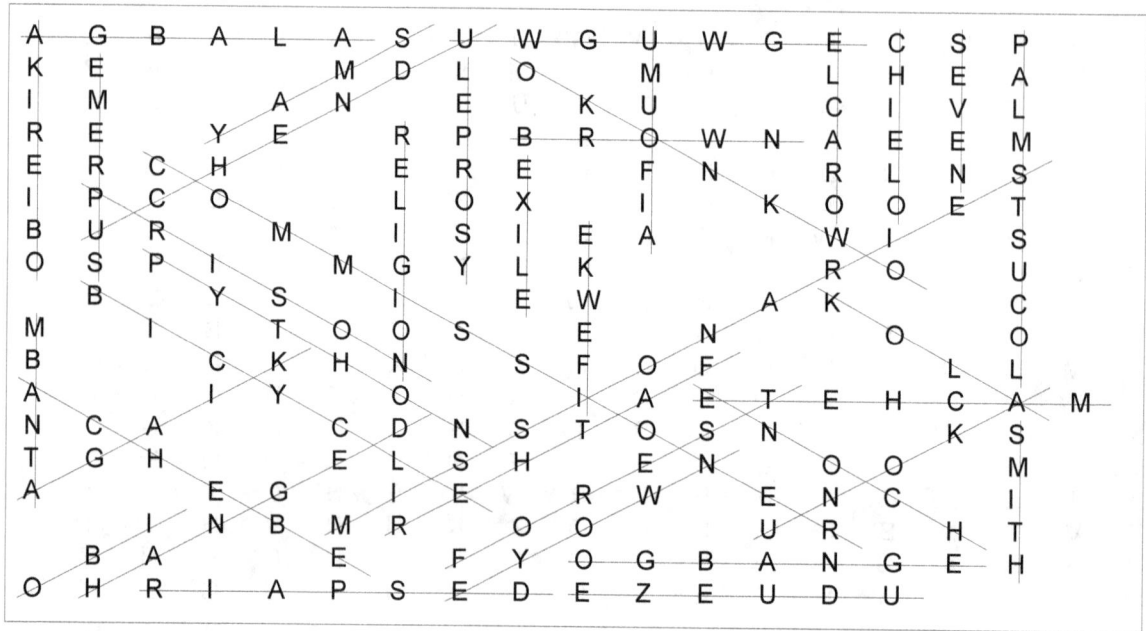

Clan translation for (7)
Author (6)
Came to convert the African natives (12)
Child who dies and returns to be reborn (7)
Clan elder who had tumultuous funeral (6)
Consulted before decisions were made by the clan (6)
Delicacy caught and roasted by villagers (7)
First missionary in Umuofia: Mr. ___ (5)
How Okonkwo killed himself (6)
In charge of the church in Umuofia after the white man left; Mr. ___ (5)
Major food crop (4)
Masqueraders who impersonate ancestral spirits (7)
Mr. Brown's unpleasant successor; Mr. ___ (5)
Number of years of Okonkwo's exile (5)
Nuts offered in hospitality (4)
Okonkwo's friend (8)
Okonkwo's home (7)
Okonkwo's punishment for accidentally shooting the boy (5)
Okonkwo's second wife and mother of Ezinma (6)
Okonkwo's son who converted to Christianity (5)

Okonkwo's unsuccessful father (5)
Oracle of the Hills and Caves (6)
Priestess of the Oracle (6)
Sacred animal (6)
Successful, strong central character of novel (7)
The iron horse (7)
Traditional dwelling or hut (3)
Type of wine the villagers drank (4)
Unmasked an egwugwu (5)
Was writing a book about his experiences in Africa (12)
Weapon Okonkwo used to kill the government messenger (7)
Welcomed Okonkwo in Mbanta (7)
What Ikemefuna called Okonkwo (6)
What Mother is, according to Uchendu (7)
What Okonkwo felt when he began his exile (7)
What white men brought, along with government (8)
Where Okonkwo and the others went for destroying the church (6)
Where Okonkwo lived in exile (6)
Where the Christians built their church; Evil ___ (6)

Things Fall Apart Word Search 3

Words are placed backwards, forward, diagonally, up and down. Words listed below are included in the maze. Circle the hidden vocabulary words in the maze.

```
T O B I E R I K A B I C Y C L E M F E D
O R K G P F Y I P G K A Y O G Z A O G N
B A P O A Y F H B A M C M M O E C R W F
I C F T N O T N B S L A H M V U H E U N
K L H I U K M H H Z L M B I E D E S G R
F E G M K R W B O A S A E S R U T T W W
R N U C S E M O B N N K E E N W E C U T
C Y G C Y V M G T T W H N I M K K Q H C
H T M O H F A E A E Z K O O E U O V E P
I I W K S E P S F Y B H C N N H L K M K
E N E V E S N I M U B D H E T C A G E W
L A D T I R O D X I N R X R J Z N Z R R
O I E X R Q I J U P T A O W Y I E M P T
M T S G W C G K D K Y H S W L G Q Q U Y
G S P N O S I R P Y D P E T N U E D S Q
P I A P C A L V W E W L S A X B N O X P
L R I L G Z E V G H I E B N E H R O X Z
Y H R A B L R N C X R G T H F P P N K Q
F C Z P Q T A Z E W O C C D E M W W Q A S
L M S P N H Y S J N V A G L O C U S T S
```

ACHEBE	EKWEFI	LEPROSY	PRISON
AGBALA	ENOCH	LOCUSTS	PYTHON
BICYCLE	EXILE	MACHETE	RELIGION
BROWN	EZEUDU	MBANTA	SEVEN
CHIELO	FATHER	NWOYE	SMITH
CHRISTIANITY	FOREST	OBI	SUPREME
CHUKWU	GOVERNMENT	OBIERIKA	UCHENDU
COMMISSIONER	HANGED	OGBANGE	UMUOFIA
COWRIES	IKEMEFUNA	OKONKWO	UNOKA
DESPAIR	KIAGA	ORACLE	WRESTLING
EGWUGWU	KOLA	PALM	YAMS

Things Fall Apart Word Search 3 Answer Key

Words are placed backwards, forward, diagonally, up and down. Words listed below are included in the maze. Circle the hidden vocabulary words in the maze.

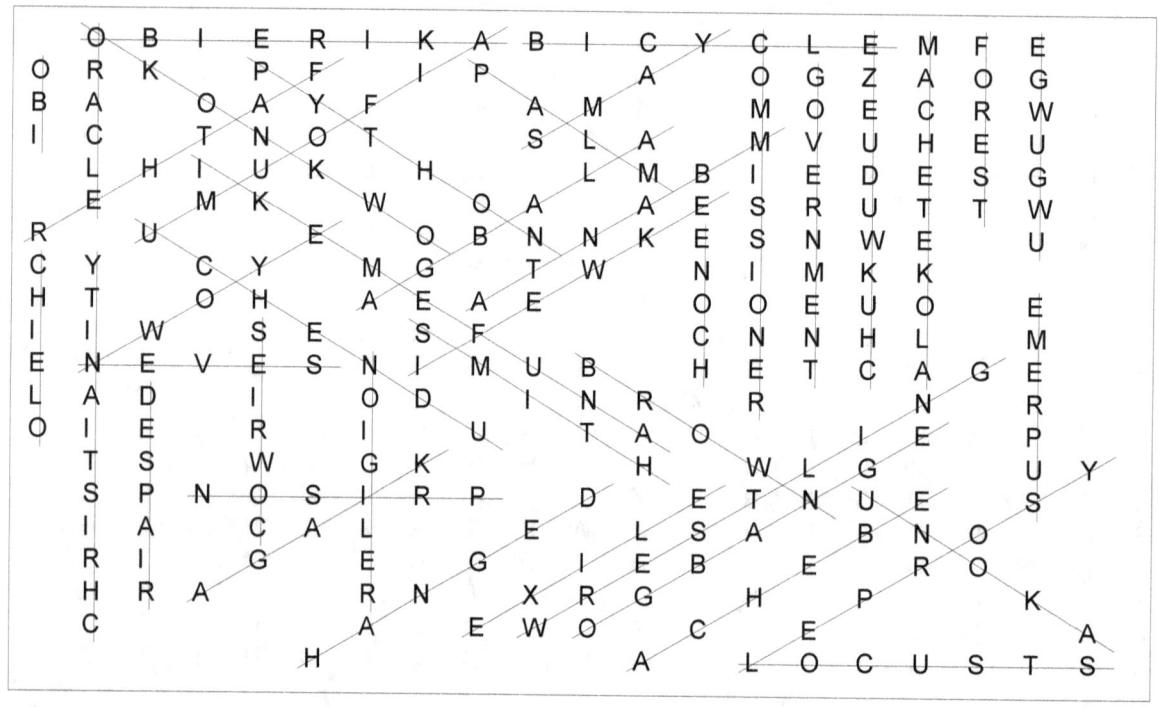

ACHEBE	EKWEFI	LEPROSY	PRISON
AGBALA	ENOCH	LOCUSTS	PYTHON
BICYCLE	EXILE	MACHETE	RELIGION
BROWN	EZEUDU	MBANTA	SEVEN
CHIELO	FATHER	NWOYE	SMITH
CHRISTIANITY	FOREST	OBI	SUPREME
CHUKWU	GOVERNMENT	OBIERIKA	UCHENDU
COMMISSIONER	HANGED	OGBANGE	UMUOFIA
COWRIES	IKEMEFUNA	OKONKWO	UNOKA
DESPAIR	KIAGA	ORACLE	WRESTLING
EGWUGWU	KOLA	PALM	YAMS

Things Fall Apart Word Search 4

Words are placed backwards, forward, diagonally, up and down. Words listed below are included in the maze. Circle the hidden vocabulary words in the maze.

```
K C H U K W U L E P R O S Y X W S C E C
S I D G V L Q N Y T R L H P R M W O N B
X F A A Q R U M U O F I A E O I Y W O V
N O I G I L E R H T I M S Z B S N R C K
Q R W B A Y X N B K A T U O I S O I H D
J E B A C K I T D C L R P C N I H E P V
D S Q L H M L S H I G O R M Y O T S M N
C T E A E M E E N S H G E L B N Y V V M
N O F V B J T G Q B L B M O Q A P A L H
N W M I E E V P P N Y A E C V R N A M Y
K G O M K N W O R B J N Z U C I P T U S
O O K Y I E Y H M P F G E S Z E B W A F
L V O Q E S M V H U R E U T M S G S T T
A E N B B K S E Z E C B D S R U F L V P
R R K J I C Z I F Y K H U V W N A O N K
W N W R C E M C O U A W E G X O T R R B
R M O B Y X R L C N N F E N D K H A R M
W E P C C T T I G C E A G F D A E C Y L
S N J N L F Q E K R J R X K I U R L N H
Y T K H E L D R I A P S E D C H I E L O
```

ACHEBE	ENOCH	LOCUSTS	PRISON
AGBALA	EXILE	MACHETE	PYTHON
BICYCLE	EZEUDU	MBANTA	RELIGION
BROWN	FATHER	MISSIONARIES	SEVEN
CHIELO	FOREST	NWOYE	SMITH
CHUKWU	GOVERNMENT	OBI	SUPREME
COMMISSIONER	HANGED	OBIERIKA	UCHENDU
COWRIES	IKEMEFUNA	OGBANGE	UMUOFIA
DESPAIR	KIAGA	OKONKWO	UNOKA
EGWUGWU	KOLA	ORACLE	WRESTLING
EKWEFI	LEPROSY	PALM	YAMS

Things Fall Apart Word Search 4 Answer Key

Words are placed backwards, forward, diagonally, up and down. Words listed below are included in the maze. Circle the hidden vocabulary words in the maze.

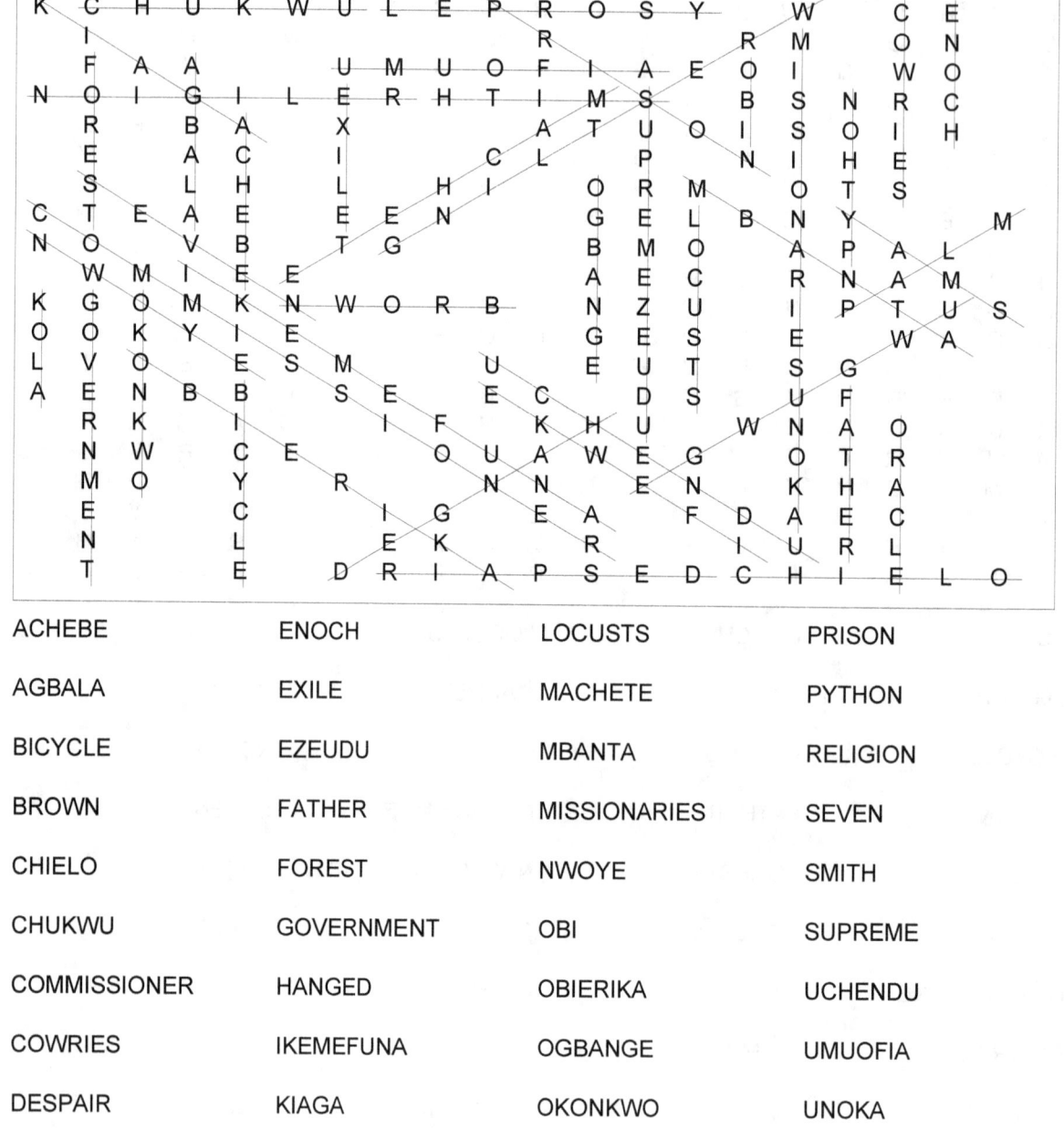

ACHEBE	ENOCH	LOCUSTS	PRISON
AGBALA	EXILE	MACHETE	PYTHON
BICYCLE	EZEUDU	MBANTA	RELIGION
BROWN	FATHER	MISSIONARIES	SEVEN
CHIELO	FOREST	NWOYE	SMITH
CHUKWU	GOVERNMENT	OBI	SUPREME
COMMISSIONER	HANGED	OBIERIKA	UCHENDU
COWRIES	IKEMEFUNA	OGBANGE	UMUOFIA
DESPAIR	KIAGA	OKONKWO	UNOKA
EGWUGWU	KOLA	ORACLE	WRESTLING
EKWEFI	LEPROSY	PALM	YAMS

Things Fall Apart Crossword 1

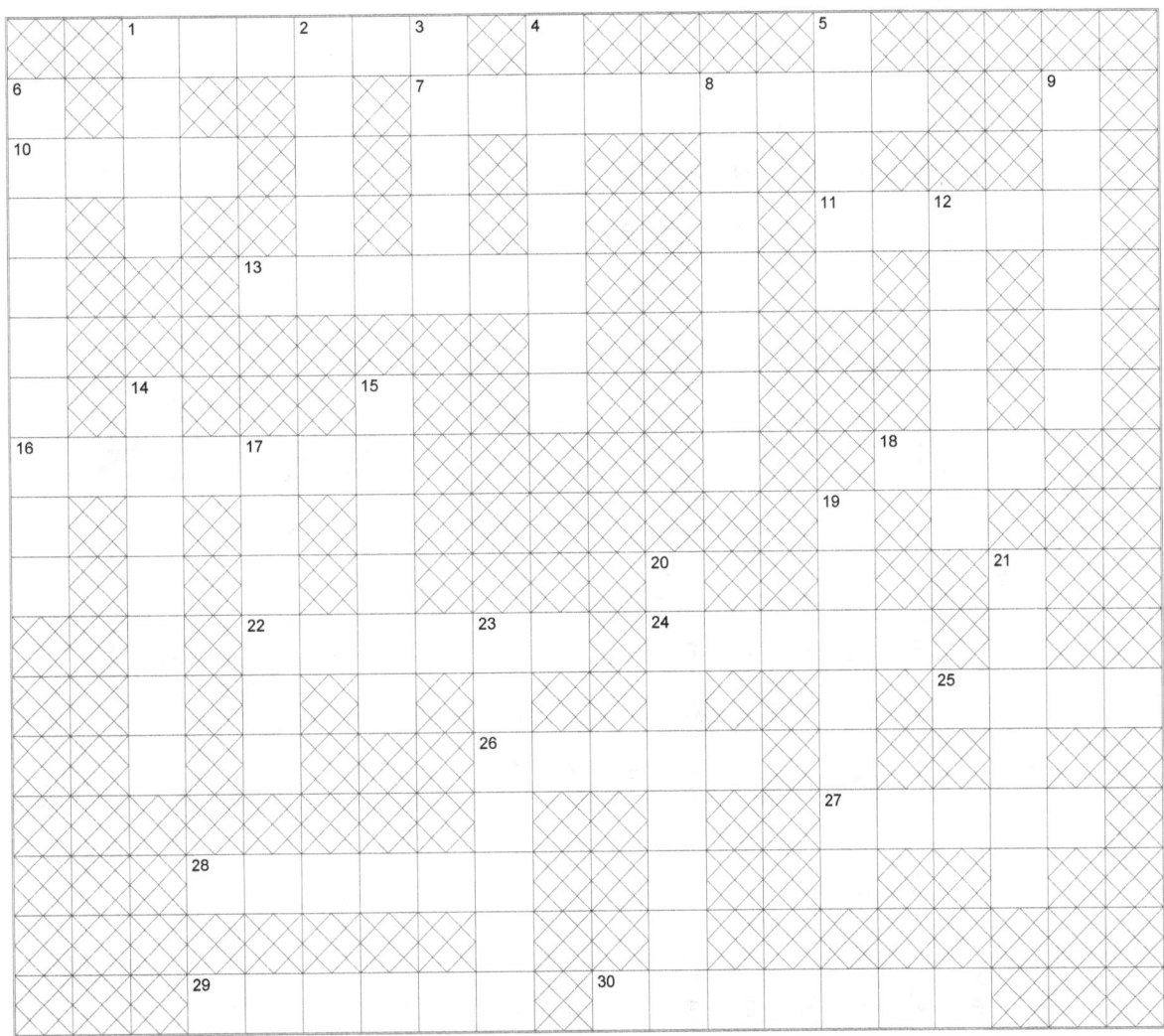

Across
1. Where Okonkwo and he others went for destroying the church
7. How Okonkwo won his early fame
10. Nuts offered in hospitality
11. In charge of the church in Umuofia after the white man left; Mr. ___
13. Priestess of the Oracle
16. Okonkwo's home
18. Traditional dwelling or hut
22. Clan elder who had tumultuous funeral
24. First missionary in Umuofia: Mr. ___
25. Major food crop
26. Number of years of Okonkwo's exile
27. Okonkwo's punishment for accidentally shooting the boy
28. Oracle of the Hills and Caves
29. What Ikemefuna called Okonkwo
30. Weapon Okonkwo used to kill the government messenger

Down
1. Type of wine the villagers drank
2. Mr. Brown's unpleasant successor; Mr. ___
3. Okonkwo's son who converted to Christianity
4. Clan translation for
5. Okonkwo's unsuccessful father
6. Murdered by the clan
8. Delicacy caught and roasted by villagers
9. Where Okonkwo lived in exile
12. Author
14. What Mother is, according to Uchendu
15. How Okonkwo killed himself
17. Where the Christians built their church; Evil ___
19. Shells used for money
20. Okonkwo's friend
21. Consulted before decisions were made by the clan
23. What Okonkwo felt when he began his exile

Things Fall Apart Crossword 1 Answer Key

		1 P	R	2 I	S	3 O	N		4 L			5 U		
6 I		A		M		7 W	R	8 E	S	T	L	I	N	9 M
10 K	O	L	A	I		O		P			O		G	B
E		M		T		Y		R			C	11 K	12 I	A	G	A
				13 C	H	I	E	L	O		U	A		C	N
E								S			S			H	T
F		14 S			15 H			Y			T			E	A
16 U	M	U	O	17 F	I	A					18 S		O	B	I
N		P		O		N						19 C		E	
A		R		R		G			20 O			O			21 O
		E		22 E	Z	E	U	23 D	U		24 B	R	O	W	N	R
		M		S				D			I			R	25 Y	A	M	S
		E		T				26 S	E	V	E	N		I		C
								P			R			27 E	X	I	L	E
		28 A	G	B	A	L	A				I			S		E
								I			K			
		29 F	A	T	H	E	R		30 M	A	C	H	E	T	E

Across
1. Where Okonkwo and he others went for destroying the church
7. How Okonkwo won his early fame
10. Nuts offered in hospitality
11. In charge of the church in Umuofia after the white man left; Mr. ___
13. Priestess of the Oracle
16. Okonkwo's home
18. Traditional dwelling or hut
22. Clan elder who had tumultuous funeral
24. First missionary in Umuofia: Mr. ___
25. Major food crop
26. Number of years of Okonkwo's exile
27. Okonkwo's punishment for accidentally shooting the boy
28. Oracle of the Hills and Caves
29. What Ikemefuna called Okonkwo
30. Weapon Okonkwo used to kill the government messenger

Down
1. Type of wine the villagers drank
2. Mr. Brown's unpleasant successor; Mr. ___
3. Okonkwo's son who converted to Christianity
4. Clan translation for
5. Okonkwo's unsuccessful father
6. Murdered by the clan
8. Delicacy caught and roasted by villagers
9. Where Okonkwo lived in exile
12. Author
14. What Mother is, according to Uchendu
15. How Okonkwo killed himself
17. Where the Christians built their church; Evil ___
19. Shells used for money
20. Okonkwo's friend
21. Consulted before decisions were made by the clan
23. What Okonkwo felt when he began his exile

Things Fall Apart Crossword 2

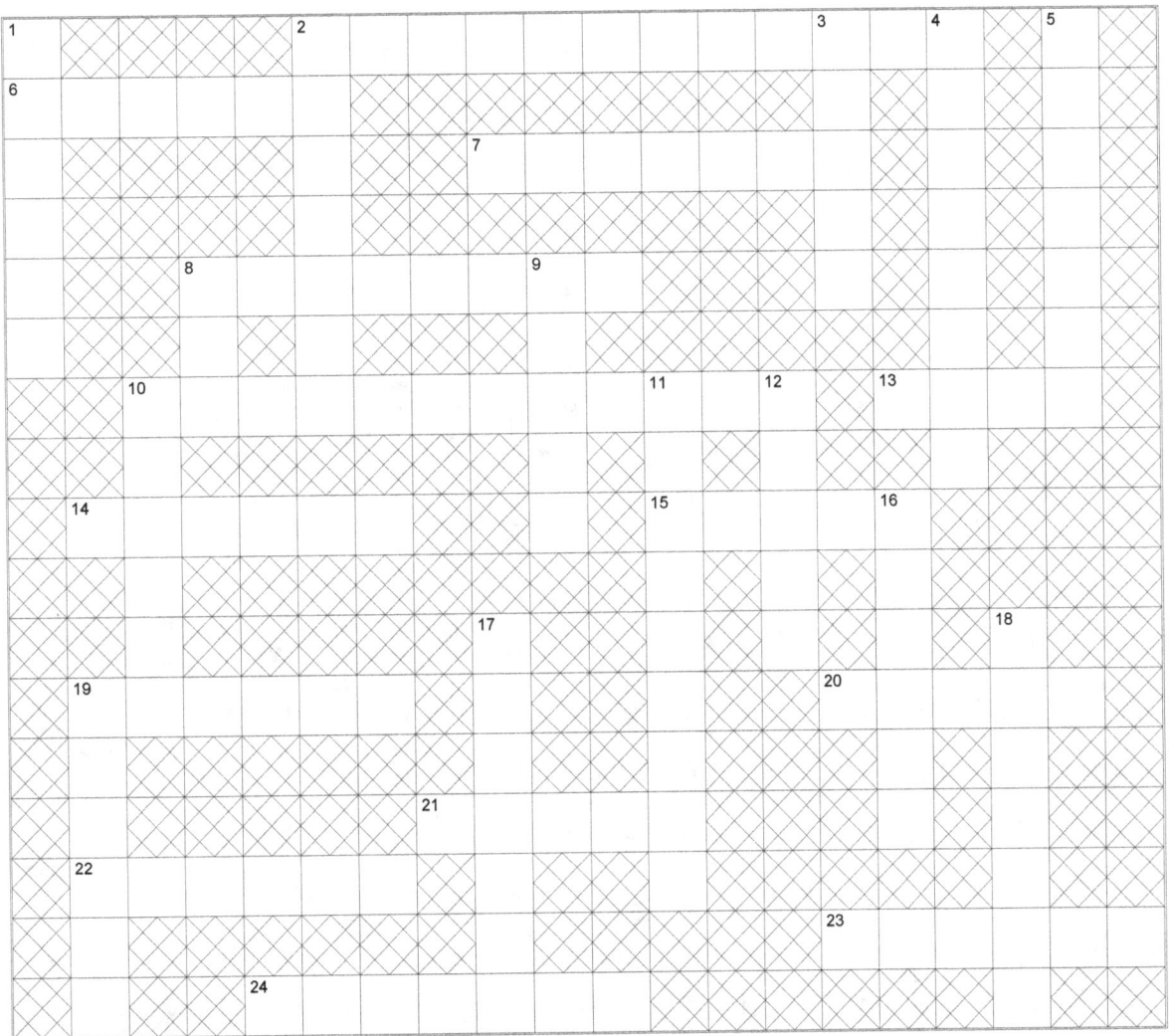

Across

2. Was writing a book about his experiences in Africa
6. Priestess of the Oracle
7. Successful, strong central character of novel
8. Okonkwo's friend
10. Came to convert the African natives
13. Nuts offered in hospitality
14. How Okonkwo killed himself
15. Okonkwo's punishment for accidentally shooting the boy
19. What Ikemefuna called Okonkwo
20. Number of years of Okonkwo's exile
21. First missionary in Umuofia: Mr. ___
22. Clan elder who had tumultuous funeral
23. Where Okonkwo and the others went for destroying the church
24. Weapon Okonkwo used to kill the government messenger

Down

1. Author
2. Shells used for money
3. Okonkwo's son who converted to Christianity
4. What white men brought, along with government
5. Okonkwo's home
8. Traditional dwelling or hut
9. In charge of the church in Umuofia after the white man left; Mr. ___
10. Where Okonkwo lived in exile
11. Murdered by the clan
12. Mr. Brown's unpleasant successor; Mr. ___
16. Okonkwo's second wife and mother of Ezinma
17. What Mother is, according to Uchendu
18. Clan translation for
19. Where the Christians built their church; Evil ___

Things Fall Apart Crossword 2 Answer Key

Across
2. Was writing a book about his experiences in Africa
6. Priestess of the Oracle
7. Successful, strong central character of novel
8. Okonkwo's friend
10. Came to convert the African natives
13. Nuts offered in hospitality
14. How Okonkwo killed himself
15. Okonkwo's punishment for accidentally shooting the boy
19. What Ikemefuna called Okonkwo
20. Number of years of Okonkwo's exile
21. First missionary in Umuofia: Mr. ___
22. Clan elder who had tumultuous funeral
23. Where Okonkwo and the others went for destroying the church
24. Weapon Okonkwo used to kill the government messenger

Down
1. Author
2. Shells used for money
3. Okonkwo's son who converted to Christianity
4. What white men brought, along with government
5. Okonkwo's home
8. Traditional dwelling or hut
9. In charge of the church in Umuofia after the white man left; Mr. ___
10. Where Okonkwo lived in exile
11. Murdered by the clan
12. Mr. Brown's unpleasant successor; Mr. ___
16. Okonkwo's second wife and mother of Ezinma
17. What Mother is, according to Uchendu
18. Clan translation for
19. Where the Christians built their church; Evil ___

Things Fall Apart Crossword 3

Across
1. The major god of the villagers
4. Mr. Brown's unpleasant successor; Mr. ___
8. Major food crop
9. What the white man brought in addition to religion
12. Traditional dwelling or hut
15. In charge of the church in Umuofia after the white man left; Mr. ___
16. First missionary in Umuofia: Mr. ___
17. Welcomed Okonkwo in Mbanta
21. Author
23. Clan elder who had tumultuous funeral
24. Type of wine the villagers drank

Down
1. Was writing a book about his experiences in Africa
2. Nuts offered in hospitality
3. Okonkwo's home
4. Number of years of Okonkwo's exile
5. Sacred animal
6. Where Okonkwo and the others went for destroying the church
7. Child who dies and returns to be reborn
10. What white men brought, along with government
11. Came to convert the African natives
13. Masqueraders who impersonate ancestral spirits
14. Weapon Okonkwo used to kill the government messenger
16. The iron horse
18. How Okonkwo killed himself
19. Okonkwo's son who converted to Christianity
20. Okonkwo's unsuccessful father
22. What Okonkwo felt when he began his exile

Things Fall Apart Crossword 3 Answer Key

Across
1. The major god of the villagers
4. Mr. Brown's unpleasant successor; Mr. ___
8. Major food crop
9. What the white man brought in addition to religion
12. Traditional dwelling or hut
15. In charge of the church in Umuofia after the white man left; Mr. ___
16. First missionary in Umuofia: Mr. ___
17. Welcomed Okonkwo in Mbanta
21. Author
23. Clan elder who had tumultuous funeral
24. Type of wine the villagers drank

Down
1. Was writing a book about his experiences in Africa
2. Nuts offered in hospitality
3. Okonkwo's home
4. Number of years of Okonkwo's exile
5. Sacred animal
6. Where Okonkwo and the others went for destroying the church
7. Child who dies and returns to be reborn
10. What white men brought, along with government
11. Came to convert the African natives
13. Masqueraders who impersonate ancestral spirits
14. Weapon Okonkwo used to kill the government messenger
16. The iron horse
18. How Okonkwo killed himself
19. Okonkwo's son who converted to Christianity
20. Okonkwo's unsuccessful father
22. What Okonkwo felt when he began his exile

Things Fall Apart Crossword 4

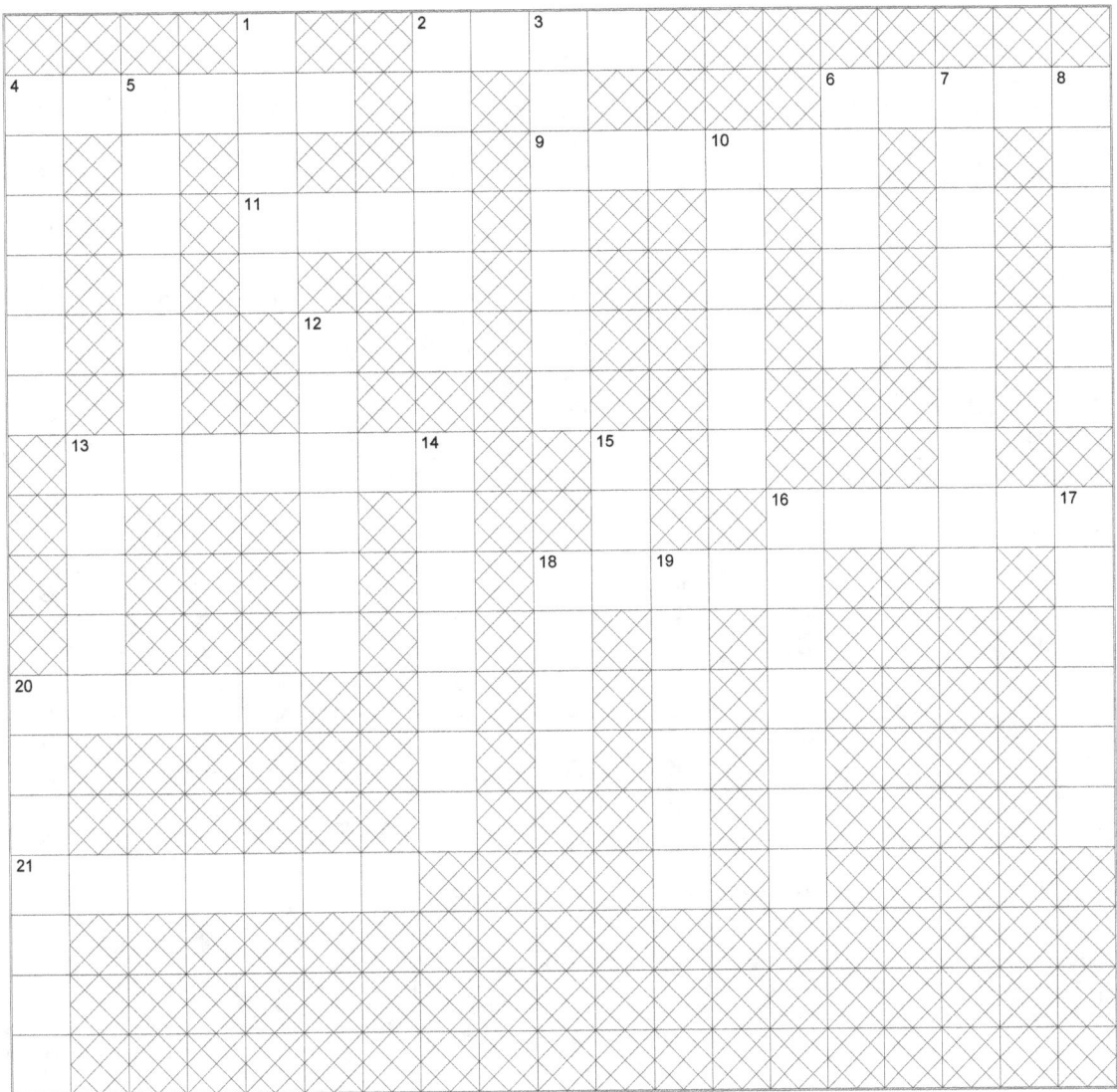

Across
2. Type of wine the villagers drank
4. The major god of the villagers
6. Okonkwo's punishment for accidentally shooting the boy
9. Sacred animal
11. Major food crop
13. What Mother is, according to Uchendu
16. Where Okonkwo lived in exile
18. In charge of the church in Umuofia after the white man left; Mr. ___
20. Okonkwo's unsuccessful father
21. Successful, strong central character of novel

Down
1. Okonkwo's son who converted to Christianity
2. Where Okonkwo and the others went for destroying the church
3. Clan translation for
4. Priestess of the Oracle
5. Welcomed Okonkwo in Mbanta
6. Unmasked an egwugwu
7. Murdered by the clan
8. Okonkwo's second wife and mother of Ezinma
10. How Okonkwo killed himself
12. Clan elder who had tumultuous funeral
13. Number of years of Okonkwo's exile
14. Masqueraders who impersonate ancestral spirits
15. Traditional dwelling or hut
16. Weapon Okonkwo used to kill the government messenger
17. Oracle of the Hills and Caves
18. Nuts offered in hospitality
19. Author
20. Okonkwo's home

Things Fall Apart Crossword 4 Answer Key

Across
2. Type of wine the villagers drank
4. The major god of the villagers
6. Okonkwo's punishment for accidentally shooting the boy
9. Sacred animal
11. Major food crop
13. What Mother is, according to Uchendu
16. Where Okonkwo lived in exile
18. In charge of the church in Umuofia after the white man left; Mr. ___
20. Okonkwo's unsuccessful father
21. Successful, strong central character of novel

Down
1. Okonkwo's son who converted to Christianity
2. Where Okonkwo and the others went for destroying the church
3. Clan translation for
4. Priestess of the Oracle
5. Welcomed Okonkwo in Mbanta
6. Unmasked an egwugwu
7. Murdered by the clan
8. Okonkwo's second wife and mother of Ezinma
10. How Okonkwo killed himself
12. Clan elder who had tumultuous funeral
13. Number of years of Okonkwo's exile
14. Masqueraders who impersonate ancestral spirits
15. Traditional dwelling or hut
16. Weapon Okonkwo used to kill the government messenger
17. Oracle of the Hills and Caves
18. Nuts offered in hospitality
19. Author
20. Okonkwo's home

Things Fall Apart

CHIELO	SUPREME	EZEUDU	UNOKA	MBANTA
LOCUSTS	KIAGA	OKONKWO	PALM	YAMS
FATHER	BROWN	FREE SPACE	WRESTLING	COMMISSIONER
GOVERNMENT	OBI	ORACLE	SEVEN	UMUOFIA
NWOYE	AGBALA	PRISON	EXILE	RELIGION

Things Fall Apart

COWRIES	MACHETE	CHUKWU	PYTHON	LEPROSY
OGBANGE	OBIERIKA	MISSIONARIES	DESPAIR	SMITH
EKWEFI	FOREST	FREE SPACE	EGWUGWU	CHRISTIANITY
ENOCH	ACHEBE	BICYCLE	KOLA	UCHENDU
RELIGION	EXILE	PRISON	AGBALA	NWOYE

Things Fall Apart

ACHEBE	WRESTLING	KOLA	ORACLE	SUPREME
RELIGION	COWRIES	OBIERIKA	OGBANGE	OKONKWO
SEVEN	MISSIONARIES	FREE SPACE	LEPROSY	PALM
CHRISTIANITY	OBI	MACHETE	BROWN	EGWUGWU
EKWEFI	UMUOFIA	GOVERNMENT	UCHENDU	BICYCLE

Things Fall Apart

YAMS	FATHER	AGBALA	SMITH	MBANTA
NWOYE	LOCUSTS	FOREST	EXILE	COMMISSIONER
IKEMEFUNA	HANGED	FREE SPACE	DESPAIR	PYTHON
CHUKWU	ENOCH	CHIELO	EZEUDU	UNOKA
BICYCLE	UCHENDU	GOVERNMENT	UMUOFIA	EKWEFI

Things Fall Apart

CHUKWU	KOLA	MBANTA	COMMISSIONER	EGWUGWU
ORACLE	WRESTLING	OKONKWO	UCHENDU	OBIERIKA
MACHETE	FOREST	FREE SPACE	KIAGA	RELIGION
LEPROSY	PYTHON	SUPREME	OGBANGE	ENOCH
AGBALA	EXILE	BROWN	EKWEFI	FATHER

Things Fall Apart

PALM	GOVERNMENT	BICYCLE	IKEMEFUNA	EZEUDU
UNOKA	OBI	CHRISTIANITY	NWOYE	SEVEN
UMUOFIA	COWRIES	FREE SPACE	SMITH	PRISON
HANGED	LOCUSTS	CHIELO	DESPAIR	YAMS
FATHER	EKWEFI	BROWN	EXILE	AGBALA

Things Fall Apart

NWOYE	OKONKWO	AGBALA	EGWUGWU	LOCUSTS
MISSIONARIES	UNOKA	KOLA	PALM	CHUKWU
EKWEFI	OGBANGE	FREE SPACE	ORACLE	EZEUDU
UMUOFIA	FATHER	PYTHON	CHIELO	WRESTLING
BICYCLE	GOVERNMENT	MACHETE	FOREST	CHRISTIANITY

Things Fall Apart

SUPREME	DESPAIR	MBANTA	ENOCH	EXILE
OBI	COMMISSIONER	KIAGA	BROWN	COWRIES
ACHEBE	SEVEN	FREE SPACE	IKEMEFUNA	PRISON
SMITH	UCHENDU	LEPROSY	HANGED	OBIERIKA
CHRISTIANITY	FOREST	MACHETE	GOVERNMENT	BICYCLE

Things Fall Apart

PALM	CHIELO	HANGED	KIAGA	WRESTLING
SUPREME	OKONKWO	ACHEBE	FATHER	NWOYE
RELIGION	KOLA	FREE SPACE	IKEMEFUNA	COWRIES
BICYCLE	EKWEFI	FOREST	BROWN	COMMISSIONER
DESPAIR	OBI	EXILE	LEPROSY	UNOKA

Things Fall Apart

LOCUSTS	PYTHON	MISSIONARIES	UCHENDU	GOVERNMENT
ORACLE	PRISON	ENOCH	CHRISTIANITY	EZEUDU
CHUKWU	YAMS	FREE SPACE	MBANTA	EGWUGWU
MACHETE	UMUOFIA	OBIERIKA	AGBALA	SEVEN
UNOKA	LEPROSY	EXILE	OBI	DESPAIR

Things Fall Apart

DESPAIR	OKONKWO	FOREST	BICYCLE	AGBALA
ENOCH	NWOYE	KOLA	UCHENDU	FATHER
GOVERNMENT	IKEMEFUNA	FREE SPACE	MACHETE	UMUOFIA
LOCUSTS	CHUKWU	SEVEN	PALM	HANGED
COMMISSIONER	UNOKA	EKWEFI	COWRIES	CHRISTIANITY

Things Fall Apart

PRISON	LEPROSY	BROWN	OBI	WRESTLING
EGWUGWU	ACHEBE	ORACLE	EXILE	SUPREME
MBANTA	OGBANGE	FREE SPACE	PYTHON	EZEUDU
CHIELO	OBIERIKA	MISSIONARIES	SMITH	KIAGA
CHRISTIANITY	COWRIES	EKWEFI	UNOKA	COMMISSIONER

Things Fall Apart

FOREST	MACHETE	ACHEBE	LOCUSTS	MISSIONARIES
EKWEFI	HANGED	COMMISSIONER	SUPREME	NWOYE
AGBALA	PYTHON	FREE SPACE	WRESTLING	COWRIES
EGWUGWU	OGBANGE	UNOKA	YAMS	BICYCLE
ORACLE	ENOCH	UCHENDU	KOLA	UMUOFIA

Things Fall Apart

IKEMEFUNA	KIAGA	EXILE	DESPAIR	OKONKWO
GOVERNMENT	MBANTA	CHUKWU	PRISON	EZEUDU
LEPROSY	CHRISTIANITY	FREE SPACE	FATHER	CHIELO
OBIERIKA	RELIGION	PALM	SMITH	SEVEN
UMUOFIA	KOLA	UCHENDU	ENOCH	ORACLE

Things Fall Apart

GOVERNMENT	UCHENDU	EZEUDU	HANGED	MBANTA
CHRISTIANITY	EKWEFI	OGBANGE	LEPROSY	FATHER
LOCUSTS	DESPAIR	FREE SPACE	KOLA	ENOCH
COMMISSIONER	FOREST	BROWN	YAMS	WRESTLING
UMUOFIA	COWRIES	OBIERIKA	NWOYE	PALM

Things Fall Apart

SEVEN	SUPREME	OKONKWO	EXILE	ORACLE
ACHEBE	UNOKA	PYTHON	RELIGION	SMITH
OBI	PRISON	FREE SPACE	CHUKWU	MACHETE
BICYCLE	EGWUGWU	AGBALA	CHIELO	MISSIONARIES
PALM	NWOYE	OBIERIKA	COWRIES	UMUOFIA

Things Fall Apart

SUPREME	COMMISSIONER	OGBANGE	DESPAIR	BROWN
ACHEBE	EGWUGWU	CHRISTIANITY	IKEMEFUNA	OKONKWO
NWOYE	RELIGION	FREE SPACE	KIAGA	PRISON
EKWEFI	LEPROSY	FOREST	YAMS	UMUOFIA
PALM	FATHER	UNOKA	BICYCLE	HANGED

Things Fall Apart

LOCUSTS	UCHENDU	WRESTLING	COWRIES	ORACLE
MISSIONARIES	OBI	GOVERNMENT	MBANTA	AGBALA
PYTHON	EZEUDU	FREE SPACE	EXILE	MACHETE
OBIERIKA	KOLA	CHUKWU	CHIELO	SMITH
HANGED	BICYCLE	UNOKA	FATHER	PALM

Things Fall Apart

OBIERIKA	MISSIONARIES	HANGED	BICYCLE	OKONKWO
KIAGA	KOLA	LOCUSTS	UNOKA	ORACLE
RELIGION	GOVERNMENT	FREE SPACE	LEPROSY	MACHETE
CHIELO	PALM	COWRIES	EZEUDU	UMUOFIA
EGWUGWU	BROWN	OGBANGE	YAMS	UCHENDU

Things Fall Apart

MBANTA	CHUKWU	OBI	AGBALA	FOREST
PYTHON	ENOCH	DESPAIR	SEVEN	FATHER
COMMISSIONER	ACHEBE	FREE SPACE	PRISON	CHRISTIANITY
EKWEFI	WRESTLING	SUPREME	EXILE	NWOYE
UCHENDU	YAMS	OGBANGE	BROWN	EGWUGWU

Things Fall Apart

BICYCLE	UCHENDU	EKWEFI	OGBANGE	IKEMEFUNA
GOVERNMENT	FOREST	UMUOFIA	ENOCH	AGBALA
PYTHON	EGWUGWU	FREE SPACE	MACHETE	OBI
NWOYE	CHRISTIANITY	PALM	FATHER	SUPREME
CHIELO	SMITH	MBANTA	CHUKWU	WRESTLING

Things Fall Apart

MISSIONARIES	HANGED	LEPROSY	EXILE	YAMS
COMMISSIONER	OBIERIKA	KOLA	ORACLE	RELIGION
UNOKA	DESPAIR	FREE SPACE	SEVEN	EZEUDU
LOCUSTS	KIAGA	BROWN	PRISON	OKONKWO
WRESTLING	CHUKWU	MBANTA	SMITH	CHIELO

Things Fall Apart

LEPROSY	EKWEFI	UMUOFIA	MACHETE	ACHEBE
WRESTLING	ORACLE	IKEMEFUNA	EGWUGWU	COWRIES
YAMS	PALM	FREE SPACE	CHUKWU	COMMISSIONER
LOCUSTS	CHIELO	MISSIONARIES	SUPREME	OBI
UCHENDU	HANGED	BICYCLE	PYTHON	KOLA

Things Fall Apart

OBIERIKA	RELIGION	PRISON	EZEUDU	OKONKWO
GOVERNMENT	CHRISTIANITY	FATHER	KIAGA	BROWN
SEVEN	UNOKA	FREE SPACE	SMITH	NWOYE
ENOCH	AGBALA	DESPAIR	OGBANGE	EXILE
KOLA	PYTHON	BICYCLE	HANGED	UCHENDU

Things Fall Apart

MISSIONARIES	SMITH	PYTHON	ACHEBE	BICYCLE
COMMISSIONER	MACHETE	WRESTLING	DESPAIR	PALM
OBIERIKA	UMUOFIA	FREE SPACE	KOLA	CHRISTIANITY
BROWN	EGWUGWU	SEVEN	NWOYE	OKONKWO
IKEMEFUNA	YAMS	EZEUDU	EXILE	KIAGA

Things Fall Apart

COWRIES	OBI	RELIGION	ENOCH	SUPREME
CHUKWU	FATHER	AGBALA	UNOKA	LEPROSY
OGBANGE	ORACLE	FREE SPACE	LOCUSTS	GOVERNMENT
EKWEFI	FOREST	HANGED	PRISON	UCHENDU
KIAGA	EXILE	EZEUDU	YAMS	IKEMEFUNA

Things Fall Apart

CHIELO	BICYCLE	IKEMEFUNA	FOREST	EZEUDU
BROWN	PRISON	SEVEN	SMITH	WRESTLING
OBIERIKA	KOLA	FREE SPACE	KIAGA	COMMISSIONER
EXILE	MBANTA	SUPREME	PYTHON	FATHER
UNOKA	EKWEFI	LOCUSTS	MISSIONARIES	UMUOFIA

Things Fall Apart

OBI	ORACLE	DESPAIR	UCHENDU	EGWUGWU
RELIGION	PALM	OKONKWO	GOVERNMENT	NWOYE
YAMS	MACHETE	FREE SPACE	CHUKWU	LEPROSY
ACHEBE	ENOCH	HANGED	AGBALA	COWRIES
UMUOFIA	MISSIONARIES	LOCUSTS	EKWEFI	UNOKA

Things Fall Apart

YAMS	LEPROSY	EXILE	EGWUGWU	MACHETE
CHIELO	OBI	UNOKA	ENOCH	FOREST
SEVEN	NWOYE	FREE SPACE	DESPAIR	GOVERNMENT
EKWEFI	OBIERIKA	RELIGION	PALM	EZEUDU
FATHER	HANGED	AGBALA	COWRIES	BROWN

Things Fall Apart

IKEMEFUNA	MBANTA	BICYCLE	PRISON	UCHENDU
SUPREME	KIAGA	KOLA	CHRISTIANITY	LOCUSTS
PYTHON	OKONKWO	FREE SPACE	SMITH	CHUKWU
MISSIONARIES	OGBANGE	UMUOFIA	WRESTLING	ORACLE
BROWN	COWRIES	AGBALA	HANGED	FATHER

Things Fall Apart

SMITH	IKEMEFUNA	HANGED	COWRIES	PYTHON
CHIELO	DESPAIR	COMMISSIONER	CHRISTIANITY	FOREST
KOLA	UMUOFIA	FREE SPACE	MACHETE	FATHER
GOVERNMENT	EZEUDU	EGWUGWU	PRISON	RELIGION
ENOCH	EKWEFI	OBIERIKA	BROWN	KIAGA

Things Fall Apart

OBI	SEVEN	MISSIONARIES	NWOYE	WRESTLING
PALM	EXILE	CHUKWU	OKONKWO	YAMS
ORACLE	LOCUSTS	FREE SPACE	OGBANGE	UNOKA
BICYCLE	SUPREME	AGBALA	LEPROSY	MBANTA
KIAGA	BROWN	OBIERIKA	EKWEFI	ENOCH

Things Fall Apart Vocabulary Word List

No.	Word	Clue/Definition
1.	ABOMINATION	Detestable things
2.	ACCOMMODATION	Help; adaptation
3.	AGITATED	Stirred up; disturbed
4.	APPROBATION	Approval
5.	BEGOT	Produced; fathered
6.	BENEVOLENT	Characterized by or suggestive of doing good
7.	BOUTS	A contest between antagonists; a match
8.	BRUSQUENESS	Abrupt and curt in manner or speech; discourteously blunt
9.	CALABASHES	Utensils or containers made from dried gourds
10.	CALLOW	Youthful; immature
11.	CAPRICIOUS	Impulsive and unpredictable
12.	COMMUNAL	Of a group of people
13.	COMPENSATION	Payment or reimbursement
14.	COMPOSURE	Mental calmness
15.	COMPROMISE	Adjustment
16.	CONSOLATIONS	Words of comfort
17.	COPIOUSLY	Abundantly
18.	CUNNING	Skill in deception; guile
19.	DELECTABLE	Delightful; delicious
20.	DERISIVE	Ridiculing
21.	DIFFUSED	Spread in all directions
22.	DISCERN	Distinguish; perceive
23.	DISCORDANT	Inharmonious; conflicting
24.	ELOQUENT	Expressive; persuasive
25.	ELUDE	Avoid; evade
26.	EMANATION	Issuing forth
27.	EMISSARY	An agent sent to represent or advance the interests of another
28.	ESOTERIC	Known only to the chosen few
29.	ESSENCES	A spiritual or incorporeal entity
30.	FEIGN	To represent falsely; pretend to
31.	FIBROUS	Threadlike
32.	FLOURISH	Grow well; prosper
33.	FRENZY	A state of violent mental agitation or wild excitement
34.	GRAVELY	Seriously
35.	HARBINGERS	One that indicates or foreshadows what is to come; a forerunner
36.	HAGGARD	Appearing worn and exhausted
37.	IMMINENT	Impending; near at hand
38.	IMPENETRABLY	Not able to be entered or pierced
39.	IMPERIOUS	Arrogantly domineering or overbearing
40.	IMPROVIDENT	Not providing for the future; thriftless; incautious
41.	INCIPIENT	Beginning to exist or appear
42.	INTERVALS	Amount of time between specified instances
43.	INTOXICATING	Stimulating or exciting
44.	KINDRED	Related to a clan or tribe
45.	LISTLESS	Lacking in spirit or energy
46.	MALEVOLENCE	Evil or harmful influence
47.	MANIFEST	Understandable; clear
48.	MIRTHLESS	Without laughter
49.	MISCREANT	Wretch; villain
50.	MUTILATE	Maim

Things Fall Apart Vocabulary Word List Continued

No.	Word	Clue/Definition
51.	NOTORIOUS	Known widely and usually unfavorably
52.	OMEN	Prophetic sign
53.	OMINOUS	Threatening
54.	OSTRACIZE	Exclude from public favor
55.	PANDEMONIUM	Wild tumult
56.	PERPETUAL	Lasting for eternity
57.	PERTURBED	Greatly disturbed
58.	PRESTIGE	Impression produced by achievement or reputation
59.	PROFOUND	Deep; complete
60.	PROVOKING	Angering; causing retaliation
61.	REBUKED	Criticized or reproved sharply; reprimanded
62.	REQUISITE	Necessary requirement
63.	RESIGNATION	Unresisting; patiently submissive
64.	RESILIENT	Elastic; able to spring back
65.	SPECIOUS	Seemingly reliable but incorrect
66.	SPECTATORS	An observer of an event
67.	STUNTED	Having growth or development stopped
68.	TUMULT	Commotion; riot
69.	VALOR	Courage and boldness, as in battle; bravery
70.	VILE	Disgusting; loathsome

Things Fall Apart Vocabulary Fill In The Blank 1

_____ 1. Utensils or containers made from dried gourds

_____ 2. Understandable; clear

_____ 3. Threadlike

_____ 4. Lacking in spirit or energy

_____ 5. Known only to the chosen few

_____ 6. Amount of time between specified instances

_____ 7. Distinguish; perceive

_____ 8. Of a group of people

_____ 9. Beginning to exist or appear

_____ 10. Issuing forth

_____ 11. Abundantly

_____ 12. A spiritual or incorporeal entity

_____ 13. Ridiculing

_____ 14. Related to a clan or tribe

_____ 15. Stirred up; disturbed

_____ 16. Having growth or development stopped

_____ 17. Not providing for the future; thriftless; incautious

_____ 18. Evil or harmful influence

_____ 19. Impulsive and unpredictable

_____ 20. Expressive; persuasive

Things Fall Apart Vocabulary Fill In The Blank 1 Answer Key

CALABASHES	1. Utensils or containers made from dried gourds
MANIFEST	2. Understandable; clear
FIBROUS	3. Threadlike
LISTLESS	4. Lacking in spirit or energy
ESOTERIC	5. Known only to the chosen few
INTERVALS	6. Amount of time between specified instances
DISCERN	7. Distinguish; perceive
COMMUNAL	8. Of a group of people
INCIPIENT	9. Beginning to exist or appear
EMANATION	10. Issuing forth
COPIOUSLY	11. Abundantly
ESSENCES	12. A spiritual or incorporeal entity
DERISIVE	13. Ridiculing
KINDRED	14. Related to a clan or tribe
AGITATED	15. Stirred up; disturbed
STUNTED	16. Having growth or development stopped
IMPROVIDENT	17. Not providing for the future; thriftless; incautious
MALEVOLENCE	18. Evil or harmful influence
CAPRICIOUS	19. Impulsive and unpredictable
ELOQUENT	20. Expressive; persuasive

Things Fall Apart Vocabulary Fill In The Blank 2

_____ 1. Distinguish; perceive

_____ 2. To represent falsely; pretend to

_____ 3. Impulsive and unpredictable

_____ 4. A spiritual or incorporeal entity

_____ 5. Avoid; evade

_____ 6. Arrogantly domineering or overbearing

_____ 7. Not able to be entered or pierced

_____ 8. Words of comfort

_____ 9. Stirred up; disturbed

_____ 10. Seemingly reliable but incorrect

_____ 11. Wild tumult

_____ 12. Without laughter

_____ 13. Threadlike

_____ 14. Commotion; riot

_____ 15. Youthful; immature

_____ 16. Related to a clan or tribe

_____ 17. Characterized by or suggestive of doing good

_____ 18. Payment or reimbursement

_____ 19. Spread in all directions

_____ 20. Seriously

Things Fall Apart Vocabulary Fill In The Blank 2 Answer Key

DISCERN	1. Distinguish; perceive
FEIGN	2. To represent falsely; pretend to
CAPRICIOUS	3. Impulsive and unpredictable
ESSENCES	4. A spiritual or incorporeal entity
ELUDE	5. Avoid; evade
IMPERIOUS	6. Arrogantly domineering or overbearing
IMPENETRABLY	7. Not able to be entered or pierced
CONSOLATIONS	8. Words of comfort
AGITATED	9. Stirred up; disturbed
SPECIOUS	10. Seemingly reliable but incorrect
PANDEMONIUM	11. Wild tumult
MIRTHLESS	12. Without laughter
FIBROUS	13. Threadlike
TUMULT	14. Commotion; riot
CALLOW	15. Youthful; immature
KINDRED	16. Related to a clan or tribe
BENEVOLENT	17. Characterized by or suggestive of doing good
COMPENSATION	18. Payment or reimbursement
DIFFUSED	19. Spread in all directions
GRAVELY	20. Seriously

Things Fall Apart Vocabulary Fill In The Blank 3

_____

_____

_____

_____

_____

_____

_____

_____

_____

_____

_____

_____

_____

_____

_____

_____

_____

_____

_____

_____

1. To represent falsely; pretend to
2. A contest between antagonists; a match
3. Approval
4. Inharmonious; conflicting
5. Avoid; evade
6. Understandable; clear
7. Youthful; immature
8. Abrupt and curt in manner or speech; discourteously blunt
9. Appearing worn and exhausted
10. Help; adaptation
11. Utensils or containers made from dried gourds
12. Not providing for the future; thriftless; incautious
13. Greatly disturbed
14. A state of violent mental agitation or wild excitement
15. Exclude from public favor
16. Issuing forth
17. Payment or reimbursement
18. An agent sent to represent or advance the interests of another
19. Ridiculing
20. Abundantly

Things Fall Apart Vocabulary Fill In The Blank 3 Answer Key

FEIGN	1. To represent falsely; pretend to
BOUTS	2. A contest between antagonists; a match
APPROBATION	3. Approval
DISCORDANT	4. Inharmonious; conflicting
ELUDE	5. Avoid; evade
MANIFEST	6. Understandable; clear
CALLOW	7. Youthful; immature
BRUSQUENESS	8. Abrupt and curt in manner or speech; discourteously blunt
HAGGARD	9. Appearing worn and exhausted
ACCOMMODATION	10. Help; adaptation
CALABASHES	11. Utensils or containers made from dried gourds
IMPROVIDENT	12. Not providing for the future; thriftless; incautious
PERTURBED	13. Greatly disturbed
FRENZY	14. A state of violent mental agitation or wild excitement
OSTRACIZE	15. Exclude from public favor
EMANATION	16. Issuing forth
COMPENSATION	17. Payment or reimbursement
EMISSARY	18. An agent sent to represent or advance the interests of another
DERISIVE	19. Ridiculing
COPIOUSLY	20. Abundantly

Things Fall Apart Vocabulary Fill In The Blank 4

_____ 1. Known widely and usually unfavorably

_____ 2. Issuing forth

_____ 3. Impulsive and unpredictable

_____ 4. Lacking in spirit or energy

_____ 5. Commotion; riot

_____ 6. Adjustment

_____ 7. Evil or harmful influence

_____ 8. Produced; fathered

_____ 9. Having growth or development stopped

_____ 10. Beginning to exist or appear

_____ 11. Skill in deception; guile

_____ 12. Spread in all directions

_____ 13. Elastic; able to spring back

_____ 14. Wild tumult

_____ 15. Abrupt and curt in manner or speech; discourteously blunt

_____ 16. Angering; causing retaliation

_____ 17. Detestable things

_____ 18. Utensils or containers made from dried gourds

_____ 19. A contest between antagonists; a match

_____ 20. Arrogantly domineering or overbearing

Things Fall Apart Vocabulary Fill In The Blank 4 Answer Key

NOTORIOUS	1. Known widely and usually unfavorably
EMANATION	2. Issuing forth
CAPRICIOUS	3. Impulsive and unpredictable
LISTLESS	4. Lacking in spirit or energy
TUMULT	5. Commotion; riot
COMPROMISE	6. Adjustment
MALEVOLENCE	7. Evil or harmful influence
BEGOT	8. Produced; fathered
STUNTED	9. Having growth or development stopped
INCIPIENT	10. Beginning to exist or appear
CUNNING	11. Skill in deception; guile
DIFFUSED	12. Spread in all directions
RESILIENT	13. Elastic; able to spring back
PANDEMONIUM	14. Wild tumult
BRUSQUENESS	15. Abrupt and curt in manner or speech; discourteously blunt
PROVOKING	16. Angering; causing retaliation
ABOMINATION	17. Detestable things
CALABASHES	18. Utensils or containers made from dried gourds
BOUTS	19. A contest between antagonists; a match
IMPERIOUS	20. Arrogantly domineering or overbearing

Things Fall Apart Vocabulary Matching 1

___ 1. CUNNING   A. Impulsive and unpredictable
___ 2. PERTURBED   B. Necessary requirement
___ 3. OSTRACIZE   C. Criticized or reproved sharply; reprimanded
___ 4. DELECTABLE   D. Skill in deception; guile
___ 5. REQUISITE   E. A spiritual or incorporeal entity
___ 6. NOTORIOUS   F. Delightful; delicious
___ 7. SPECIOUS   G. Lacking in spirit or energy
___ 8. COMPROMISE   H. Characterized by or suggestive of doing good
___ 9. MIRTHLESS   I. Greatly disturbed
___ 10. CALLOW   J. Help; adaptation
___ 11. MUTILATE   K. Impending; near at hand
___ 12. CAPRICIOUS   L. Seemingly reliable but incorrect
___ 13. PANDEMONIUM   M. Known widely and usually unfavorably
___ 14. DIFFUSED   N. Known only to the chosen few
___ 15. BENEVOLENT   O. Arrogantly domineering or overbearing
___ 16. DISCORDANT   P. Without laughter
___ 17. REBUKED   Q. Wild tumult
___ 18. IMPENETRABLY   R. Adjustment
___ 19. IMPERIOUS   S. Maim
___ 20. ESOTERIC   T. Spread in all directions
___ 21. IMMINENT   U. Exclude from public favor
___ 22. FEIGN   V. To represent falsely; pretend to
___ 23. ACCOMMODATION   W. Not able to be entered or pierced
___ 24. LISTLESS   X. Inharmonious; conflicting
___ 25. ESSENCES   Y. Youthful; immature

Things Fall Apart Vocabulary Matching 1 Answer Key

D - 1. CUNNING	A.	Impulsive and unpredictable
I - 2. PERTURBED	B.	Necessary requirement
U - 3. OSTRACIZE	C.	Criticized or reproved sharply; reprimanded
F - 4. DELECTABLE	D.	Skill in deception; guile
B - 5. REQUISITE	E.	A spiritual or incorporeal entity
M - 6. NOTORIOUS	F.	Delightful; delicious
L - 7. SPECIOUS	G.	Lacking in spirit or energy
R - 8. COMPROMISE	H.	Characterized by or suggestive of doing good
P - 9. MIRTHLESS	I.	Greatly disturbed
Y - 10. CALLOW	J.	Help; adaptation
S - 11. MUTILATE	K.	Impending; near at hand
A - 12. CAPRICIOUS	L.	Seemingly reliable but incorrect
Q - 13. PANDEMONIUM	M.	Known widely and usually unfavorably
T - 14. DIFFUSED	N.	Known only to the chosen few
H - 15. BENEVOLENT	O.	Arrogantly domineering or overbearing
X - 16. DISCORDANT	P.	Without laughter
C - 17. REBUKED	Q.	Wild tumult
W - 18. IMPENETRABLY	R.	Adjustment
O - 19. IMPERIOUS	S.	Maim
N - 20. ESOTERIC	T.	Spread in all directions
K - 21. IMMINENT	U.	Exclude from public favor
V - 22. FEIGN	V.	To represent falsely; pretend to
J - 23. ACCOMMODATION	W.	Not able to be entered or pierced
G - 24. LISTLESS	X.	Inharmonious; conflicting
E - 25. ESSENCES	Y.	Youthful; immature

Things Fall Apart Vocabulary Matching 2

___ 1. COMPOSURE   A. Characterized by or suggestive of doing good
___ 2. EMANATION   B. Approval
___ 3. DIFFUSED   C. Seemingly reliable but incorrect
___ 4. NOTORIOUS   D. Produced; fathered
___ 5. FLOURISH   E. Courage and boldness, as in battle; bravery
___ 6. SPECIOUS   F. Grow well; prosper
___ 7. COPIOUSLY   G. Wretch; villain
___ 8. DELECTABLE   H. Not providing for the future; thriftless; incautious
___ 9. BEGOT   I. Impending; near at hand
___ 10. MUTILATE   J. Understandable; clear
___ 11. IMMINENT   K. Spread in all directions
___ 12. COMMUNAL   L. Issuing forth
___ 13. EMISSARY   M. Youthful; immature
___ 14. ACCOMMODATION   N. Arrogantly domineering or overbearing
___ 15. IMPROVIDENT   O. Avoid; evade
___ 16. CUNNING   P. Skill in deception; guile
___ 17. VALOR   Q. Abundantly
___ 18. CALLOW   R. Known only to the chosen few
___ 19. IMPERIOUS   S. Maim
___ 20. BENEVOLENT   T. Mental calmness
___ 21. ELUDE   U. Known widely and usually unfavorably
___ 22. APPROBATION   V. Help; adaptation
___ 23. MANIFEST   W. Of a group of people
___ 24. ESOTERIC   X. Delightful; delicious
___ 25. MISCREANT   Y. An agent sent to represent or advance the interests of another

Things Fall Apart Vocabulary Matching 2 Answer Key

T - 1. COMPOSURE	A. Characterized by or suggestive of doing good
L - 2. EMANATION	B. Approval
K - 3. DIFFUSED	C. Seemingly reliable but incorrect
U - 4. NOTORIOUS	D. Produced; fathered
F - 5. FLOURISH	E. Courage and boldness, as in battle; bravery
C - 6. SPECIOUS	F. Grow well; prosper
Q - 7. COPIOUSLY	G. Wretch; villain
X - 8. DELECTABLE	H. Not providing for the future; thriftless; incautious
D - 9. BEGOT	I. Impending; near at hand
S - 10. MUTILATE	J. Understandable; clear
I - 11. IMMINENT	K. Spread in all directions
W - 12. COMMUNAL	L. Issuing forth
Y - 13. EMISSARY	M. Youthful; immature
V - 14. ACCOMMODATION	N. Arrogantly domineering or overbearing
H - 15. IMPROVIDENT	O. Avoid; evade
P - 16. CUNNING	P. Skill in deception; guile
E - 17. VALOR	Q. Abundantly
M - 18. CALLOW	R. Known only to the chosen few
N - 19. IMPERIOUS	S. Maim
A - 20. BENEVOLENT	T. Mental calmness
O - 21. ELUDE	U. Known widely and usually unfavorably
B - 22. APPROBATION	V. Help; adaptation
J - 23. MANIFEST	W. Of a group of people
R - 24. ESOTERIC	X. Delightful; delicious
G - 25. MISCREANT	Y. An agent sent to represent or advance the interests of another

Things Fall Apart Vocabulary Matching 3

___ 1. OMINOUS
___ 2. BEGOT
___ 3. SPECIOUS
___ 4. DIFFUSED
___ 5. MISCREANT
___ 6. ELUDE
___ 7. ELOQUENT
___ 8. COMPENSATION
___ 9. HAGGARD
___ 10. INCIPIENT
___ 11. ESSENCES
___ 12. GRAVELY
___ 13. COMMUNAL
___ 14. COMPROMISE
___ 15. IMPERIOUS
___ 16. BOUTS
___ 17. REQUISITE
___ 18. MANIFEST
___ 19. REBUKED
___ 20. CALABASHES
___ 21. PROFOUND
___ 22. EMISSARY
___ 23. MUTILATE
___ 24. INTERVALS
___ 25. SPECTATORS

A. Seemingly reliable but incorrect
B. Produced; fathered
C. Criticized or reproved sharply; reprimanded
D. Of a group of people
E. Expressive; persuasive
F. An agent sent to represent or advance the interests of another
G. Understandable; clear
H. Appearing worn and exhausted
I. Deep; complete
J. A contest between antagonists; a match
K. Arrogantly domineering or overbearing
L. A spiritual or incorporeal entity
M. Amount of time between specified instances
N. Avoid; evade
O. Adjustment
P. Spread in all directions
Q. Necessary requirement
R. Wretch; villain
S. Seriously
T. Payment or reimbursement
U. Beginning to exist or appear
V. An observer of an event
W. Threatening
X. Utensils or containers made from dried gourds
Y. Maim

Things Fall Apart Vocabulary Matching 3 Answer Key

W - 1. OMINOUS	A.	Seemingly reliable but incorrect
B - 2. BEGOT	B.	Produced; fathered
A - 3. SPECIOUS	C.	Criticized or reproved sharply; reprimanded
P - 4. DIFFUSED	D.	Of a group of people
R - 5. MISCREANT	E.	Expressive; persuasive
N - 6. ELUDE	F.	An agent sent to represent or advance the interests of another
E - 7. ELOQUENT	G.	Understandable; clear
T - 8. COMPENSATION	H.	Appearing worn and exhausted
H - 9. HAGGARD	I.	Deep; complete
U - 10. INCIPIENT	J.	A contest between antagonists; a match
L - 11. ESSENCES	K.	Arrogantly domineering or overbearing
S - 12. GRAVELY	L.	A spiritual or incorporeal entity
D - 13. COMMUNAL	M.	Amount of time between specified instances
O - 14. COMPROMISE	N.	Avoid; evade
K - 15. IMPERIOUS	O.	Adjustment
J - 16. BOUTS	P.	Spread in all directions
Q - 17. REQUISITE	Q.	Necessary requirement
G - 18. MANIFEST	R.	Wretch; villain
C - 19. REBUKED	S.	Seriously
X - 20. CALABASHES	T.	Payment or reimbursement
I - 21. PROFOUND	U.	Beginning to exist or appear
F - 22. EMISSARY	V.	An observer of an event
Y - 23. MUTILATE	W.	Threatening
M - 24. INTERVALS	X.	Utensils or containers made from dried gourds
V - 25. SPECTATORS	Y.	Maim

Things Fall Apart Vocabulary Matching 4

___ 1. KINDRED   A. Impending; near at hand
___ 2. IMPERIOUS   B. Threadlike
___ 3. FIBROUS   C. Abundantly
___ 4. COMPENSATION   D. Expressive; persuasive
___ 5. MANIFEST   E. Stirred up; disturbed
___ 6. IMMINENT   F. Arrogantly domineering or overbearing
___ 7. REBUKED   G. Payment or reimbursement
___ 8. PROFOUND   H. Understandable; clear
___ 9. COMPROMISE   I. Characterized by or suggestive of doing good
___ 10. CONSOLATIONS   J. Skill in deception; guile
___ 11. TUMULT   K. Deep; complete
___ 12. REQUISITE   L. Youthful; immature
___ 13. ELOQUENT   M. Courage and boldness, as in battle; bravery
___ 14. AGITATED   N. Criticized or reproved sharply; reprimanded
___ 15. MUTILATE   O. An agent sent to represent or advance the interests of another
___ 16. ACCOMMODATION   P. Without laughter
___ 17. CUNNING   Q. Grow well; prosper
___ 18. COPIOUSLY   R. Necessary requirement
___ 19. VALOR   S. Maim
___ 20. CALLOW   T. Words of comfort
___ 21. EMISSARY   U. Adjustment
___ 22. FLOURISH   V. Commotion; riot
___ 23. MIRTHLESS   W. Related to a clan or tribe
___ 24. BENEVOLENT   X. Avoid; evade
___ 25. ELUDE   Y. Help; adaptation

Things Fall Apart Vocabulary Matching 4 Answer Key

W - 1. KINDRED	A.	Impending; near at hand
F - 2. IMPERIOUS	B.	Threadlike
B - 3. FIBROUS	C.	Abundantly
G - 4. COMPENSATION	D.	Expressive; persuasive
H - 5. MANIFEST	E.	Stirred up; disturbed
A - 6. IMMINENT	F.	Arrogantly domineering or overbearing
N - 7. REBUKED	G.	Payment or reimbursement
K - 8. PROFOUND	H.	Understandable; clear
U - 9. COMPROMISE	I.	Characterized by or suggestive of doing good
T - 10. CONSOLATIONS	J.	Skill in deception; guile
V - 11. TUMULT	K.	Deep; complete
R - 12. REQUISITE	L.	Youthful; immature
D - 13. ELOQUENT	M.	Courage and boldness, as in battle; bravery
E - 14. AGITATED	N.	Criticized or reproved sharply; reprimanded
S - 15. MUTILATE	O.	An agent sent to represent or advance the interests of another
Y - 16. ACCOMMODATION	P.	Without laughter
J - 17. CUNNING	Q.	Grow well; prosper
C - 18. COPIOUSLY	R.	Necessary requirement
M - 19. VALOR	S.	Maim
L - 20. CALLOW	T.	Words of comfort
O - 21. EMISSARY	U.	Adjustment
Q - 22. FLOURISH	V.	Commotion; riot
P - 23. MIRTHLESS	W.	Related to a clan or tribe
I - 24. BENEVOLENT	X.	Avoid; evade
X - 25. ELUDE	Y.	Help; adaptation

Things Fall Apart Vocabulary Magic Squares 1

Match the definition with the vocabulary word. Put your answers in the magic squares below. When your answers are correct, all columns and rows will add to the same number.

A. PROVOKING
B. FEIGN
C. ABOMINATION
D. COMPENSATION
E. ELUDE
F. FLOURISH
G. CONSOLATIONS
H. HAGGARD
I. VALOR
J. IMMINENT
K. MISCREANT
L. MUTILATE
M. HARBINGERS
N. INCIPIENT
O. OSTRACIZE
P. INTOXICATING

1. To represent falsely; pretend to
2. Words of comfort
3. Wretch; villain
4. Beginning to exist or appear
5. One that indicates or foreshadows what is to come; a forerunner
6. Maim
7. Appearing worn and exhausted
8. Angering; causing retaliation
9. Stimulating or exciting
10. Courage and boldness, as in battle; bravery
11. Avoid; evade
12. Payment or reimbursement
13. Detestable things
14. Grow well; prosper
15. Impending; near at hand
16. Exclude from public favor

A=	B=	C=	D=
E=	F=	G=	H=
I=	J=	K=	L=
M=	N=	O=	P=

Things Fall Apart Vocabulary Magic Squares 1 Answer Key

Match the definition with the vocabulary word. Put your answers in the magic squares below. When your answers are correct, all columns and rows will add to the same number.

A. PROVOKING
B. FEIGN
C. ABOMINATION
D. COMPENSATION
E. ELUDE
F. FLOURISH
G. CONSOLATIONS
H. HAGGARD
I. VALOR
J. IMMINENT
K. MISCREANT
L. MUTILATE
M. HARBINGERS
N. INCIPIENT
O. OSTRACIZE
P. INTOXICATING

1. To represent falsely; pretend to
2. Words of comfort
3. Wretch; villain
4. Beginning to exist or appear
5. One that indicates or foreshadows what is to come; a forerunner
6. Maim
7. Appearing worn and exhausted
8. Angering; causing retaliation
9. Stimulating or exciting
10. Courage and boldness, as in battle; bravery
11. Avoid; evade
12. Payment or reimbursement
13. Detestable things
14. Grow well; prosper
15. Impending; near at hand
16. Exclude from public favor

A=8	B=1	C=13	D=12
E=11	F=14	G=2	H=7
I=10	J=15	K=3	L=6
M=5	N=4	O=16	P=9

Things Fall Apart Vocabulary Magic Squares 2

Match the definition with the vocabulary word. Put your answers in the magic squares below. When your answers are correct, all columns and rows will add to the same number.

A. IMPROVIDENT
B. CONSOLATIONS
C. ABOMINATION
D. EMANATION
E. GRAVELY
F. BOUTS
G. COMPOSURE
H. LISTLESS
I. FEIGN
J. HARBINGERS
K. CALLOW
L. REBUKED
M. PERPETUAL
N. HAGGARD
O. RESIGNATION
P. COMMUNAL

1. Unresisting; patiently submissive
2. Issuing forth
3. One that indicates or foreshadows what is to come; a forerunner
4. Seriously
5. To represent falsely; pretend to
6. A contest between antagonists; a match
7. Of a group of people
8. Detestable things
9. Lacking in spirit or energy
10. Youthful; immature
11. Not providing for the future; thriftless; incautious
12. Appearing worn and exhausted
13. Words of comfort
14. Lasting for eternity
15. Mental calmness
16. Criticized or reproved sharply; reprimanded

A=	B=	C=	D=
E=	F=	G=	H=
I=	J=	K=	L=
M=	N=	O=	P=

Things Fall Apart Vocabulary Magic Squares 2 Answer Key

Match the definition with the vocabulary word. Put your answers in the magic squares below. When your answers are correct, all columns and rows will add to the same number.

A. IMPROVIDENT
B. CONSOLATIONS
C. ABOMINATION
D. EMANATION
E. GRAVELY
F. BOUTS
G. COMPOSURE
H. LISTLESS
I. FEIGN
J. HARBINGERS
K. CALLOW
L. REBUKED
M. PERPETUAL
N. HAGGARD
O. RESIGNATION
P. COMMUNAL

1. Unresisting; patiently submissive
2. Issuing forth
3. One that indicates or foreshadows what is to come; a forerunner
4. Seriously
5. To represent falsely; pretend to
6. A contest between antagonists; a match
7. Of a group of people
8. Detestable things
9. Lacking in spirit or energy
10. Youthful; immature
11. Not providing for the future; thriftless; incautious
12. Appearing worn and exhausted
13. Words of comfort
14. Lasting for eternity
15. Mental calmness
16. Criticized or reproved sharply; reprimanded

A=11	B=13	C=8	D=2
E=4	F=6	G=15	H=9
I=5	J=3	K=10	L=16
M=14	N=12	O=1	P=7

Things Fall Apart Vocabulary Magic Squares 3

Match the definition with the vocabulary word. Put your answers in the magic squares below. When your answers are correct, all columns and rows will add to the same number.

A. CUNNING
B. COMPROMISE
C. PANDEMONIUM
D. HAGGARD
E. COPIOUSLY
F. EMISSARY
G. ELOQUENT
H. INCIPIENT
I. CAPRICIOUS
J. FLOURISH
K. AGITATED
L. COMMUNAL
M. CALABASHES
N. DELECTABLE
O. KINDRED
P. REQUISITE

1. Wild tumult
2. Grow well; prosper
3. An agent sent to represent or advance the interests of another
4. Related to a clan or tribe
5. Necessary requirement
6. Abundantly
7. Impulsive and unpredictable
8. Appearing worn and exhausted
9. Utensils or containers made from dried gourds
10. Beginning to exist or appear
11. Of a group of people
12. Skill in deception; guile
13. Adjustment
14. Stirred up; disturbed
15. Expressive; persuasive
16. Delightful; delicious

A=	B=	C=	D=
E=	F=	G=	H=
I=	J=	K=	L=
M=	N=	O=	P=

Things Fall Apart Vocabulary Magic Squares 3 Answer Key

Match the definition with the vocabulary word. Put your answers in the magic squares below. When your answers are correct, all columns and rows will add to the same number.

A. CUNNING
B. COMPROMISE
C. PANDEMONIUM
D. HAGGARD
E. COPIOUSLY
F. EMISSARY
G. ELOQUENT
H. INCIPIENT
I. CAPRICIOUS
J. FLOURISH
K. AGITATED
L. COMMUNAL
M. CALABASHES
N. DELECTABLE
O. KINDRED
P. REQUISITE

1. Wild tumult
2. Grow well; prosper
3. An agent sent to represent or advance the interests of another
4. Related to a clan or tribe
5. Necessary requirement
6. Abundantly
7. Impulsive and unpredictable
8. Appearing worn and exhausted
9. Utensils or containers made from dried gourds
10. Beginning to exist or appear
11. Of a group of people
12. Skill in deception; guile
13. Adjustment
14. Stirred up; disturbed
15. Expressive; persuasive
16. Delightful; delicious

A=12	B=13	C=1	D=8
E=6	F=3	G=15	H=10
I=7	J=2	K=14	L=11
M=9	N=16	O=4	P=5

Things Fall Apart Vocabulary Magic Squares 4

Match the definition with the vocabulary word. Put your answers in the magic squares below. When your answers are correct, all columns and rows will add to the same number.

A. HAGGARD
B. DELECTABLE
C. EMISSARY
D. INTOXICATING
E. TUMULT
F. ELOQUENT
G. COMPROMISE
H. PROFOUND
I. EMANATION
J. MUTILATE
K. BEGOT
L. GRAVELY
M. INTERVALS
N. BRUSQUENESS
O. MALEVOLENCE
P. VILE

1. Amount of time between specified instances
2. Expressive; persuasive
3. Deep; complete
4. Evil or harmful influence
5. Seriously
6. An agent sent to represent or advance the interests of another
7. Appearing worn and exhausted
8. Maim
9. Produced; fathered
10. Stimulating or exciting
11. Delightful; delicious
12. Issuing forth
13. Abrupt and curt in manner or speech; discourteously blunt
14. Commotion; riot
15. Adjustment
16. Disgusting; loathsome

A=	B=	C=	D=
E=	F=	G=	H=
I=	J=	K=	L=
M=	N=	O=	P=

Things Fall Apart Vocabulary Magic Squares 4 Answer Key

Match the definition with the vocabulary word. Put your answers in the magic squares below. When your answers are correct, all columns and rows will add to the same number.

A. HAGGARD
B. DELECTABLE
C. EMISSARY
D. INTOXICATING
E. TUMULT
F. ELOQUENT
G. COMPROMISE
H. PROFOUND
I. EMANATION
J. MUTILATE
K. BEGOT
L. GRAVELY
M. INTERVALS
N. BRUSQUENESS
O. MALEVOLENCE
P. VILE

1. Amount of time between specified instances
2. Expressive; persuasive
3. Deep; complete
4. Evil or harmful influence
5. Seriously
6. An agent sent to represent or advance the interests of another
7. Appearing worn and exhausted
8. Maim
9. Produced; fathered
10. Stimulating or exciting
11. Delightful; delicious
12. Issuing forth
13. Abrupt and curt in manner or speech; discourteously blunt
14. Commotion; riot
15. Adjustment
16. Disgusting; loathsome

A=7	B=11	C=6	D=10
E=14	F=2	G=15	H=3
I=12	J=8	K=9	L=5
M=1	N=13	O=4	P=16

Things Fall Apart Vocabulary Word Search 1

Words are placed backwards, forward, diagonally, up and down. Clues listed below can help you find the words. Circle the hidden vocabulary words in the maze.

```
G E M I S S A R Y R E S I L I E N T C C
H R M L N X B Z O B K V M S U O R B I F
A S A Y D P X M F I S C M E L R S N R H
G G N V F E I G N B N O I T A N A M E B
G R I C E N Y D M E G M N I N W L D T R
A W F N O L R D K G Q P E S U H N Y O H
R Q E U M E Y X O O L R N I M Y P P S Y
D G S M D J Z S S T M O T U M V B E E Y
I I T I D D N R T M U M W Q O P C Z T Y
N S N S E W E O R Y T I Z E C N D S N Q
T P P C R X R T A C I S N R E I L C E F
O E R R I D F A C K L E V L S X V L U W
X C E E S P Y T I H A M O C R D I V Q W
I I S A I V I C Z Z T V E S D S C A O T
C O T N V I L E E P E R P E T U A L L X
A U I T E T D P N L N S K L N U L O E K
T S G S S U Z S A T T U E N Z A N R N K
I M E N L N E M O U B S I Z C F W T M T
N J P E Y J V B O E S N E S S E N C E S
G T U M U L T B R A G I T A T E D M C D
```

Adjustment (10)
A contest between antagonists; a match (5)
A spiritual or incorporeal entity (8)
A state of violent mental agitation or wild excitement (6)
An agent sent to represent or advance the interests of another (8)
An observer of an event (10)
Appearing worn and exhausted (7)
Avoid; evade (5)
Beginning to exist or appear (9)
Commotion; riot (6)
Courage and boldness, as in battle; bravery (5)
Criticized or reproved sharply; reprimanded (7)
Disgusting; loathsome (4)
Distinguish; perceive (7)
Elastic; able to spring back (9)
Evil or harmful influence (11)
Exclude from public favor (9)
Expressive; persuasive (8)
Having growth or development stopped (7)
Impending; near at hand (8)
Impression produced by achievement or reputation (8)

Issuing forth (9)
Known only to the chosen few (8)
Lacking in spirit or energy (8)
Lasting for eternity (9)
Maim (8)
Necessary requirement (9)
Of a group of people (8)
Produced; fathered (5)
Prophetic sign (4)
Related to a clan or tribe (7)
Ridiculing (8)
Seemingly reliable but incorrect (8)
Seriously (7)
Skill in deception; guile (7)
Stimulating or exciting (12)
Stirred up; disturbed (8)
Threadlike (7)
Threatening (7)
To represent falsely; pretend to (5)
Understandable; clear (8)
Wretch; villain (9)
Youthful; immature (6)

Things Fall Apart Vocabulary Word Search 1 Answer Key

Words are placed backwards, forward, diagonally, up and down. Clues listed below can help you find the words. Circle the hidden vocabulary words in the maze.

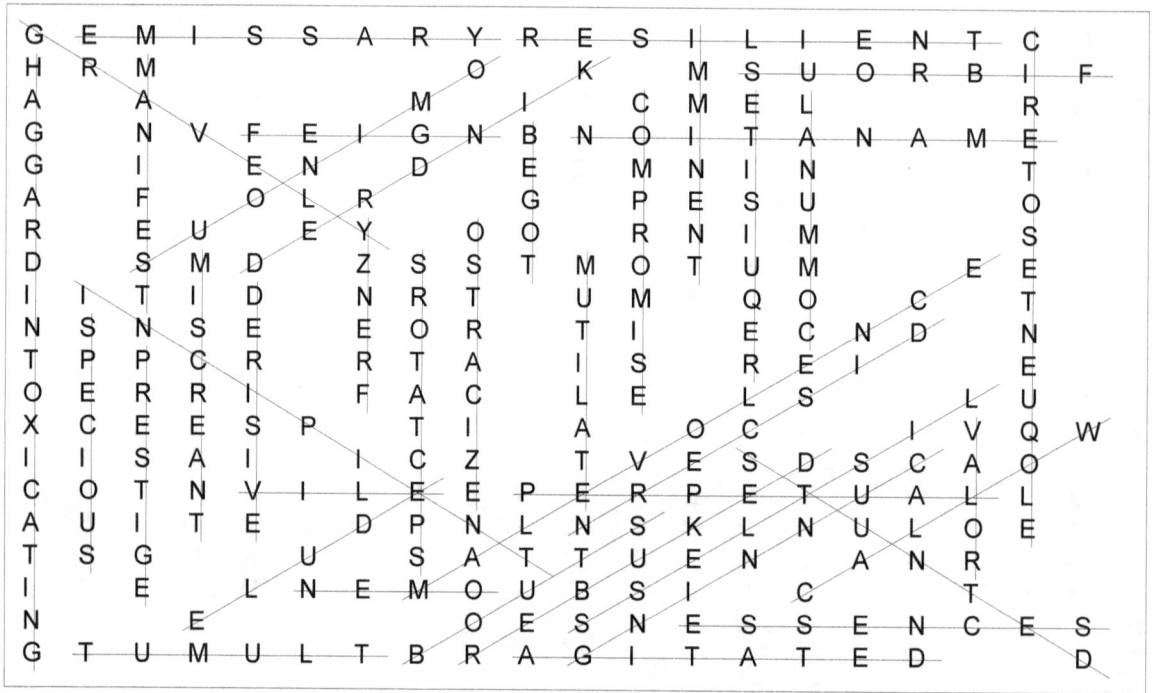

Adjustment (10)
A contest between antagonists; a match (5)
A spiritual or incorporeal entity (8)
A state of violent mental agitation or wild excitement (6)
An agent sent to represent or advance the interests of another (8)
An observer of an event (10)
Appearing worn and exhausted (7)
Avoid; evade (5)
Beginning to exist or appear (9)
Commotion; riot (6)
Courage and boldness, as in battle; bravery (5)
Criticized or reproved sharply; reprimanded (7)
Disgusting; loathsome (4)
Distinguish; perceive (7)
Elastic; able to spring back (9)
Evil or harmful influence (11)
Exclude from public favor (9)
Expressive; persuasive (8)
Having growth or development stopped (7)
Impending; near at hand (8)
Impression produced by achievement or reputation (8)

Issuing forth (9)
Known only to the chosen few (8)
Lacking in spirit or energy (8)
Lasting for eternity (9)
Maim (8)
Necessary requirement (9)
Of a group of people (8)
Produced; fathered (5)
Prophetic sign (4)
Related to a clan or tribe (7)
Ridiculing (8)
Seemingly reliable but incorrect (8)
Seriously (7)
Skill in deception; guile (7)
Stimulating or exciting (12)
Stirred up; disturbed (8)
Threadlike (7)
Threatening (7)
To represent falsely; pretend to (5)
Understandable; clear (8)
Wretch; villain (9)
Youthful; immature (6)

Things Fall Apart Vocabulary Word Search 2

Words are placed backwards, forward, diagonally, up and down. Clues listed below can help you find the words. Circle the hidden vocabulary words in the maze.

```
R E B U K E D C O M P O S U R E Q Y N R
C D I S C E R N J S S U O I R O T O N R
S T U N T E D F E T H H N T Q M I Y B P
H A G G A R D H R S T T B O U T S X L X
R Y R T V R S A V E E Y R W A G T A M F
L T E N R A C F C R N M C N K T N R U W
N L S Y B I V T V I S Z A N F U L S I H
Y E I A Z P I A D N R M Y E M X N Q N T
M A L E V O L E N C E S I M O R P M O C
Y A I O Z S E F H I G S O O W R M G M T
C I E M Q M S L F P N C O B D X E C E K
F M N P G U S H R I I C U T D B X P D H
L M T R W B E D Q E B X V N E Y E A N J
O I S E C N N N C N R R H R N R G C A S
U N S S A X C W T T A Z O H T I I F P C
R E M T L F E I G N H L E U T B N C M L
I N F I L B S N L P A D R A S Q G G V B
S T D G O E G X H V U B T U M U L T R N
H R K E W L S G Z L E E M I S S A R Y Z
D F D I F F U S E D D E R I S I V E S L
```

Adjustment (10)
A contest between antagonists; a match (5)
A spiritual or incorporeal entity (8)
A state of violent mental agitation or wild excitement (6)
Amount of time between specified instances (9)
An agent sent to represent or advance the interests of another (8)
Appearing worn and exhausted (7)
Avoid; evade (5)
Beginning to exist or appear (9)
Commotion; riot (6)
Courage and boldness, as in battle; bravery (5)
Criticized or reproved sharply; reprimanded (7)
Disgusting; loathsome (4)
Distinguish; perceive (7)
Elastic; able to spring back (9)
Evil or harmful influence (11)
Exclude from public favor (9)
Expressive; persuasive (8)
Greatly disturbed (9)
Grow well; prosper (8)
Having growth or development stopped (7)
Impending; near at hand (8)

Impression produced by achievement or reputation (8)
Issuing forth (9)
Known only to the chosen few (8)
Known widely and usually unfavorably (9)
Lacking in spirit or energy (8)
Mental calmness (9)
Of a group of people (8)
One that indicates or foreshadows what is to come; a forerunner (10)
Produced; fathered (5)
Prophetic sign (4)
Ridiculing (8)
Skill in deception; guile (7)
Spread in all directions (8)
Stirred up; disturbed (8)
Threadlike (7)
To represent falsely; pretend to (5)
Utensils or containers made from dried gourds (10)
Wild tumult (11)
Youthful; immature (6)

Things Fall Apart Vocabulary Word Search 2 Answer Key

Words are placed backwards, forward, diagonally, up and down. Clues listed below can help you find the words. Circle the hidden vocabulary words in the maze.

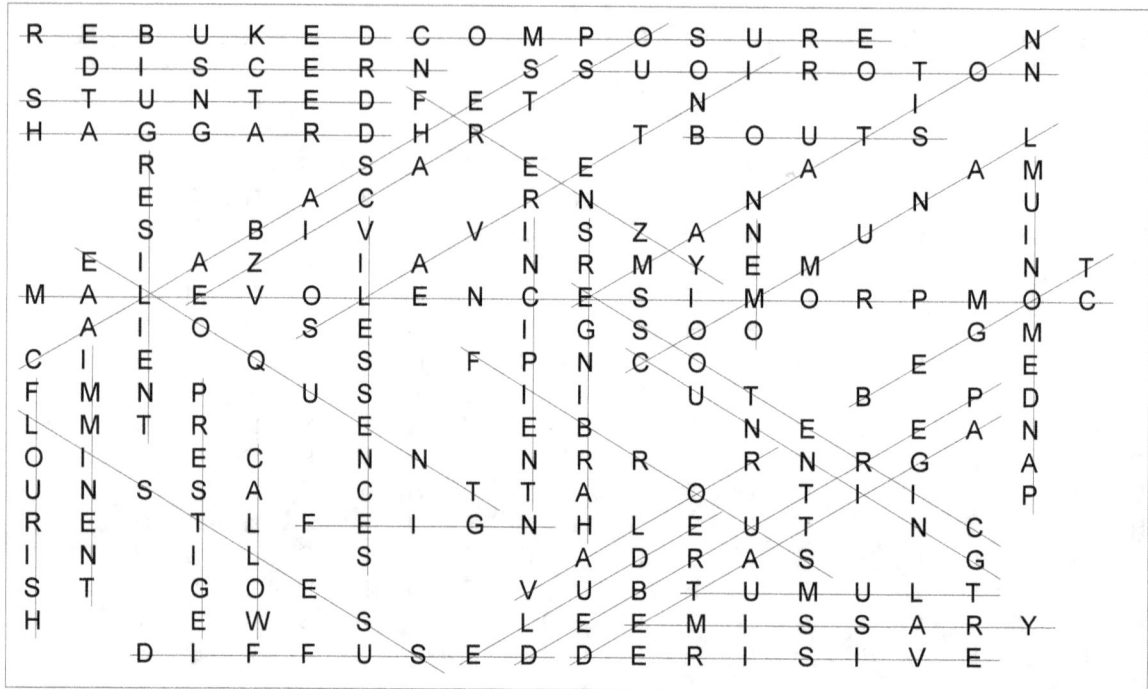

Adjustment (10)
A contest between antagonists; a match (5)
A spiritual or incorporeal entity (8)
A state of violent mental agitation or wild excitement (6)
Amount of time between specified instances (9)
An agent sent to represent or advance the interests of another (8)
Appearing worn and exhausted (7)
Avoid; evade (5)
Beginning to exist or appear (9)
Commotion; riot (6)
Courage and boldness, as in battle; bravery (5)
Criticized or reproved sharply; reprimanded (7)
Disgusting; loathsome (4)
Distinguish; perceive (7)
Elastic; able to spring back (9)
Evil or harmful influence (11)
Exclude from public favor (9)
Expressive; persuasive (8)
Greatly disturbed (9)
Grow well; prosper (8)
Having growth or development stopped (7)
Impending; near at hand (8)

Impression produced by achievement or reputation (8)
Issuing forth (9)
Known only to the chosen few (8)
Known widely and usually unfavorably (9)
Lacking in spirit or energy (8)
Mental calmness (9)
Of a group of people (8)
One that indicates or foreshadows what is to come; a forerunner (10)
Produced; fathered (5)
Prophetic sign (4)
Ridiculing (8)
Skill in deception; guile (7)
Spread in all directions (8)
Stirred up; disturbed (8)
Threadlike (7)
To represent falsely; pretend to (5)
Utensils or containers made from dried gourds (10)
Wild tumult (11)
Youthful; immature (6)

Things Fall Apart Vocabulary Word Search 3

Words are placed backwards, forward, diagonally, up and down. Words listed below are included in the maze. Circle the hidden vocabulary words in the maze.

```
A G I T A T E D R A G G A H Z W C G I F
G C E M I N C I P I E N T L O I O R N R
J I S E P M A N I F E S T L L M M A T T
P R S M D E T N U T S W L S J P P V O C
X E E I I F R J L N R A D T N R E E X L
C T N S F R K I C D C T K R K O N L I Z
N O C S I E T H O R G N P N I V S Y C T
D S E A B N E H E U C A R K N I A B A V
V E S R R Z L Q L N S E D S D D T O T P
M A R Y O Y U D K E C R V Y R E I U I K
D U L I U I D V B S S C L S E N O T N Y
E F T O S P E C I O U S R R D T N S G S
S Y Y I R I U D M L U I P E O N R L B F
U N T X L N V H M O E M R G B E L A Z P
F E I G N A T E I T O M E N T U B V G N
F C M I P H T P N F H B S I U Q K R Q W
I C N B Z Y O E E H V G T B M O G E D S
D G R Y Q C D Q N G T N I R U L H T D G
F L O U R I S H T D F Y G A L E W N T P
I M P E N E T R A B L Y E H T J W I F S
```

AGITATED	ELUDE	IMMINENT	MUTILATE
BEGOT	EMISSARY	IMPENETRABLY	OMEN
BOUTS	ESOTERIC	IMPERIOUS	PRESTIGE
CALLOW	ESSENCES	IMPROVIDENT	REBUKED
COMPENSATION	FEIGN	INCIPIENT	REQUISITE
COPIOUSLY	FIBROUS	INTERVALS	SPECIOUS
CUNNING	FLOURISH	INTOXICATING	STUNTED
DERISIVE	FRENZY	KINDRED	TUMULT
DIFFUSED	GRAVELY	MANIFEST	VALOR
DISCERN	HAGGARD	MIRTHLESS	VILE
ELOQUENT	HARBINGERS	MISCREANT	

Things Fall Apart Vocabulary Word Search 3 Answer Key

Words are placed backwards, forward, diagonally, up and down. Words listed below are included in the maze. Circle the hidden vocabulary words in the maze.

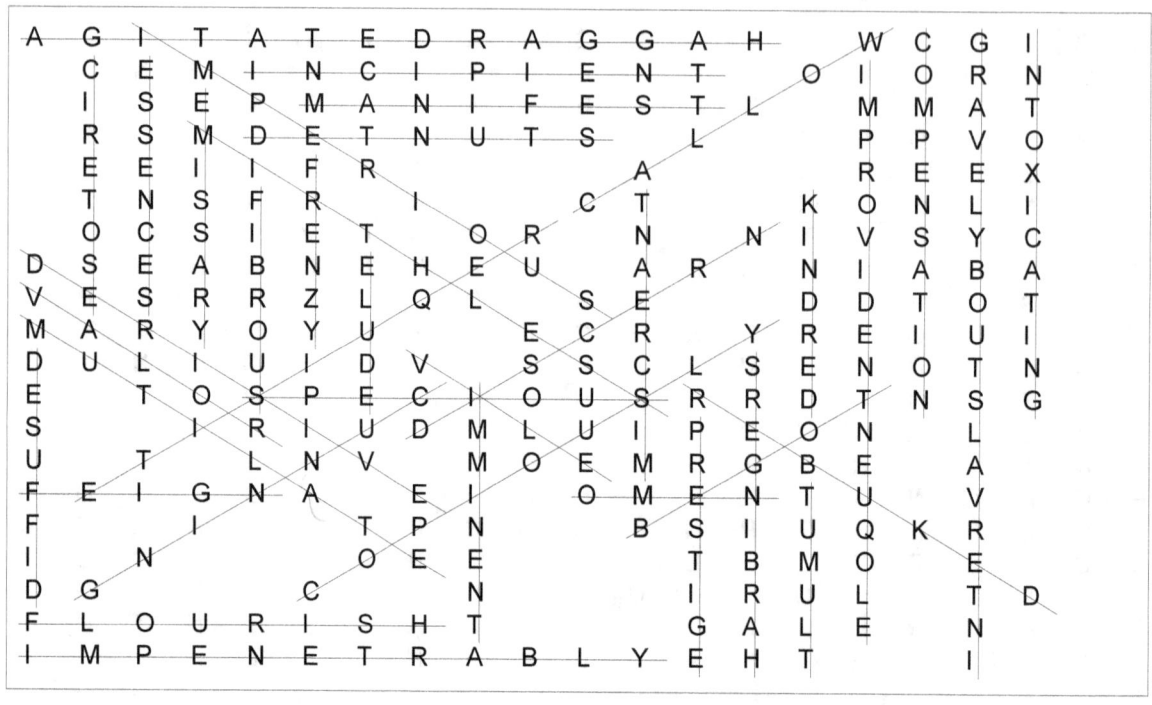

AGITATED	ELUDE	IMMINENT	MUTILATE
BEGOT	EMISSARY	IMPENETRABLY	OMEN
BOUTS	ESOTERIC	IMPERIOUS	PRESTIGE
CALLOW	ESSENCES	IMPROVIDENT	REBUKED
COMPENSATION	FEIGN	INCIPIENT	REQUISITE
COPIOUSLY	FIBROUS	INTERVALS	SPECIOUS
CUNNING	FLOURISH	INTOXICATING	STUNTED
DERISIVE	FRENZY	KINDRED	TUMULT
DIFFUSED	GRAVELY	MANIFEST	VALOR
DISCERN	HAGGARD	MIRTHLESS	VILE
ELOQUENT	HARBINGERS	MISCREANT	

Things Fall Apart Vocabulary Word Search 4

Words are placed backwards, forward, diagonally, up and down. Words listed below are included in the maze. Circle the hidden vocabulary words in the maze.

```
O S T R A C I Z E D S S E L H T R I M J
R M B C O M P O S U R E M C A N D R L J
E U I E W C K D O O T P A U R N K F R N
S T F N G B G N T Q D M N N B K Y K G H
I I I T O O W A E W A C A N I J Q R P R
L L B G H U T C R N Y O T I N D A C E D
I A R W N C S B I M D P I N G V D M R G
E T O Y E J R F C E I I O G E B I S T N
N E U P W O E Y T T S O N L R S D S U F
T F S C L S M A S W C U Y X S J E E R R
L C E A T F T F U P E S S A P S S L B S
B Y V I W I B V O S R L R P R S U T E Y
R E S I G N A T I O N Y Z N E R F S D P
B R L A E N F M C L D G L N S C F I T Z
M Y W D M W O M I E E M C B T Z I L U C
K P U N O R D N R B Z E V J I L D O M B
K L S L P Z P D P O S H A G G A R D U J
E Q L M Y P N L A U T E P R E P W W L S
F A O D N I P F C T N E U Q O L E K T R
C C D E K U B E R S T U N T E D O M E N
```

AGITATED	ELOQUENT	HARBINGERS	PRESTIGE
BEGOT	ELUDE	KINDRED	REBUKED
BOUTS	EMANATION	LISTLESS	RESIGNATION
CALLOW	EMISSARY	MANIFEST	RESILIENT
CAPRICIOUS	ESOTERIC	MIRTHLESS	SPECIOUS
COMPOSURE	ESSENCES	MUTILATE	SPECTATORS
COMPROMISE	FEIGN	OMEN	STUNTED
COPIOUSLY	FIBROUS	OMINOUS	TUMULT
CUNNING	FRENZY	OSTRACIZE	VALOR
DIFFUSED	GRAVELY	PERPETUAL	VILE
DISCERN	HAGGARD	PERTURBED	

Things Fall Apart Vocabulary Word Search 4 Answer Key

Words are placed backwards, forward, diagonally, up and down. Words listed below are included in the maze. Circle the hidden vocabulary words in the maze.

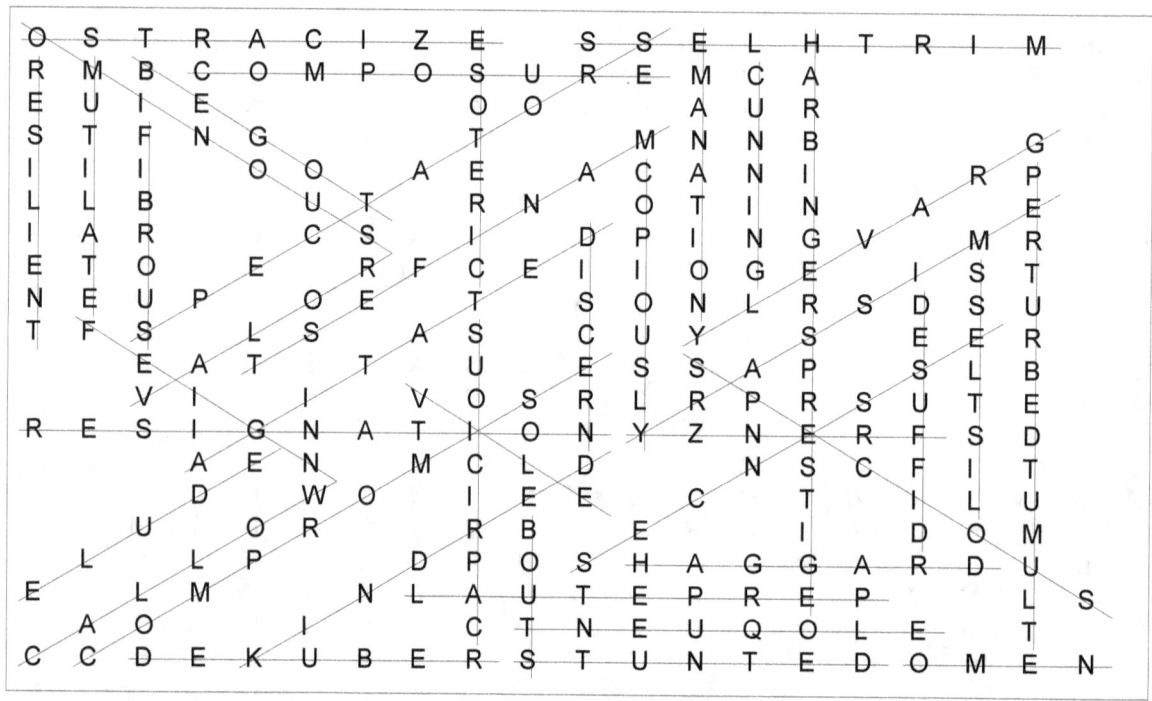

AGITATED	ELOQUENT	HARBINGERS	PRESTIGE
BEGOT	ELUDE	KINDRED	REBUKED
BOUTS	EMANATION	LISTLESS	RESIGNATION
CALLOW	EMISSARY	MANIFEST	RESILIENT
CAPRICIOUS	ESOTERIC	MIRTHLESS	SPECIOUS
COMPOSURE	ESSENCES	MUTILATE	SPECTATORS
COMPROMISE	FEIGN	OMEN	STUNTED
COPIOUSLY	FIBROUS	OMINOUS	TUMULT
CUNNING	FRENZY	OSTRACIZE	VALOR
DIFFUSED	GRAVELY	PERPETUAL	VILE
DISCERN	HAGGARD	PERTURBED	

Things Fall Apart Vocabulary Crossword 1

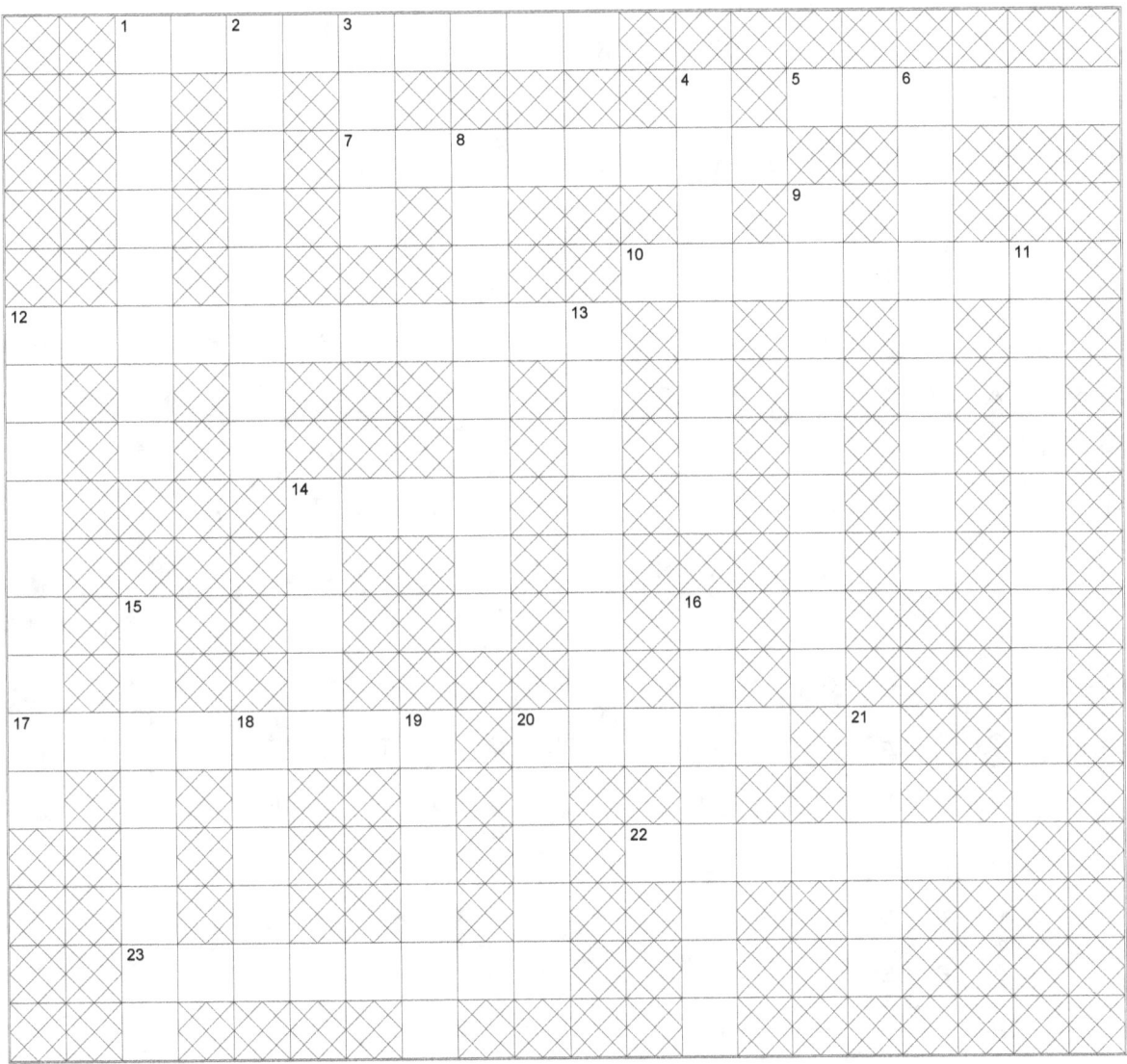

Across
1. Mental calmness
5. Commotion; riot
7. An agent sent to represent or advance the interests of another
10. A spiritual or incorporeal entity
12. Wild tumult
14. Disgusting; loathsome
17. Known only to the chosen few
20. Produced; fathered
22. Skill in deception; guile
23. Seemingly reliable but incorrect

Down
1. Of a group of people
2. Understandable; clear
3. Prophetic sign
4. Impression produced by achievement or reputation
6. Wretch; villain
8. Beginning to exist or appear
9. Elastic; able to spring back
11. An observer of an event
12. Greatly disturbed
13. Maim
14. Courage and boldness, as in battle; bravery
15. Grow well; prosper
16. Expressive; persuasive
18. Avoid; evade
19. Youthful; immature
20. A contest between antagonists; a match
21. To represent falsely; pretend to

Things Fall Apart Vocabulary Crossword 1 Answer Key

Across
1. Mental calmness
5. Commotion; riot
7. An agent sent to represent or advance the interests of another
10. A spiritual or incorporeal entity
12. Wild tumult
14. Disgusting; loathsome
17. Known only to the chosen few
20. Produced; fathered
22. Skill in deception; guile
23. Seemingly reliable but incorrect

Down
1. Of a group of people
2. Understandable; clear
3. Prophetic sign
4. Impression produced by achievement or reputation
6. Wretch; villain
8. Beginning to exist or appear
9. Elastic; able to spring back
11. An observer of an event
12. Greatly disturbed
13. Maim
14. Courage and boldness, as in battle; bravery
15. Grow well; prosper
16. Expressive; persuasive
18. Avoid; evade
19. Youthful; immature
20. A contest between antagonists; a match
21. To represent falsely; pretend to

Things Fall Apart Vocabulary Crossword 2

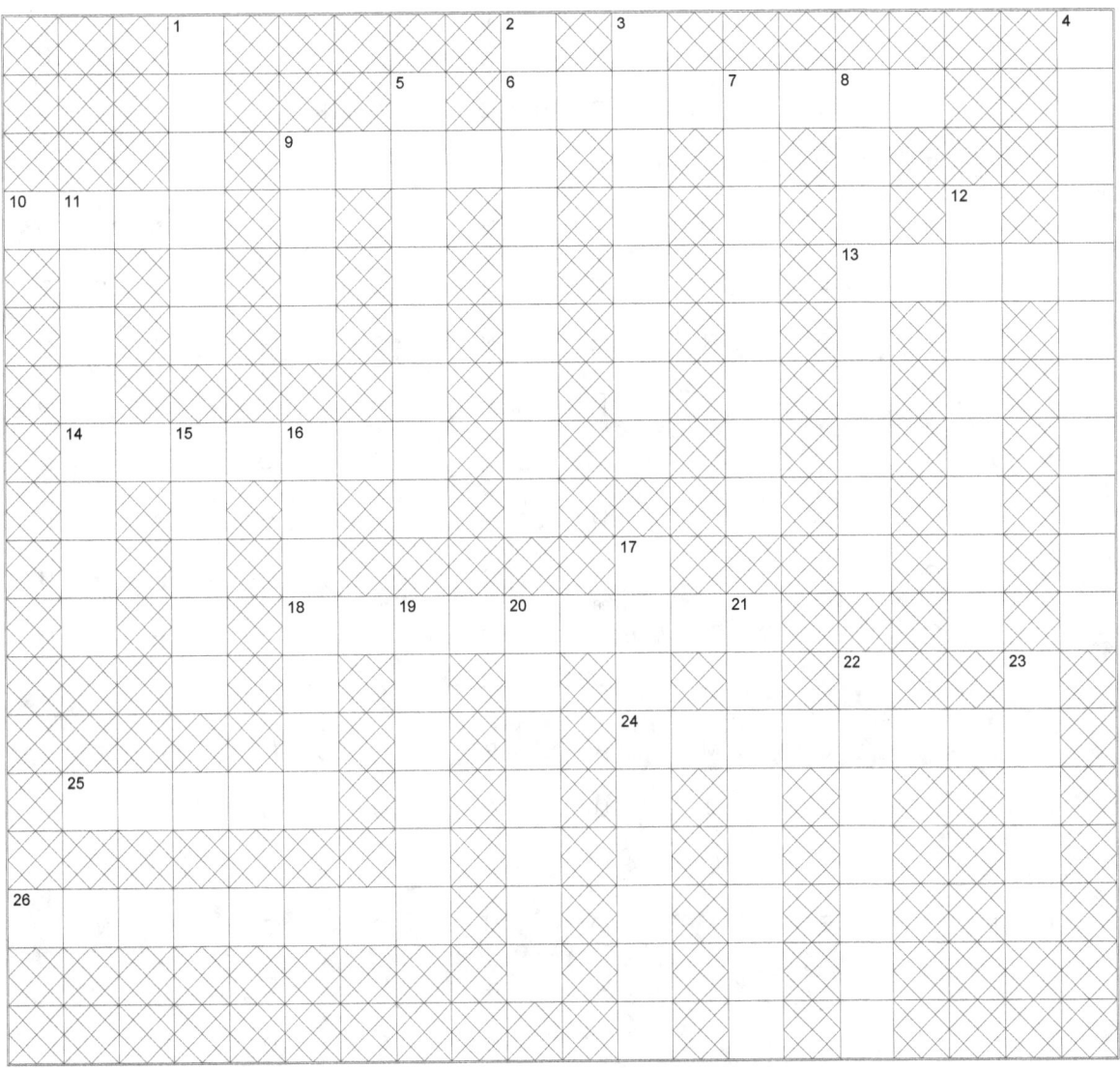

Across
6. Known only to the chosen few
9. Courage and boldness, as in battle; bravery
10. Prophetic sign
13. Avoid; evade
14. Threadlike
18. Known widely and usually unfavorably
24. Impression produced by achievement or reputation
25. A contest between antagonists; a match
26. Impending; near at hand

Down
1. A state of violent mental agitation or wild excitement
2. Greatly disturbed
3. Of a group of people
4. Wild tumult
5. Grow well; prosper
7. An agent sent to represent or advance the interests of another
8. Arrogantly domineering or overbearing
9. Disgusting; loathsome
11. Understandable; clear
12. Maim
15. Produced; fathered
16. Threatening
17. Mental calmness
19. Commotion; riot
20. Criticized or reproved sharply; reprimanded
21. Seemingly reliable but incorrect
22. Having growth or development stopped
23. To represent falsely; pretend to

Things Fall Apart Vocabulary Crossword 2 Answer Key

Across
6. Known only to the chosen few
9. Courage and boldness, as in battle; bravery
10. Prophetic sign
13. Avoid; evade
14. Threadlike
18. Known widely and usually unfavorably
24. Impression produced by achievement or reputation
25. A contest between antagonists; a match
26. Impending; near at hand

Down
1. A state of violent mental agitation or wild excitement
2. Greatly disturbed
3. Of a group of people
4. Wild tumult
5. Grow well; prosper
7. An agent sent to represent or advance the interests of another
8. Arrogantly domineering or overbearing
9. Disgusting; loathsome
11. Understandable; clear
12. Maim
15. Produced; fathered
16. Threatening
17. Mental calmness
19. Commotion; riot
20. Criticized or reproved sharply; reprimanded
21. Seemingly reliable but incorrect
22. Having growth or development stopped
23. To represent falsely; pretend to

Things Fall Apart Vocabulary Crossword 3

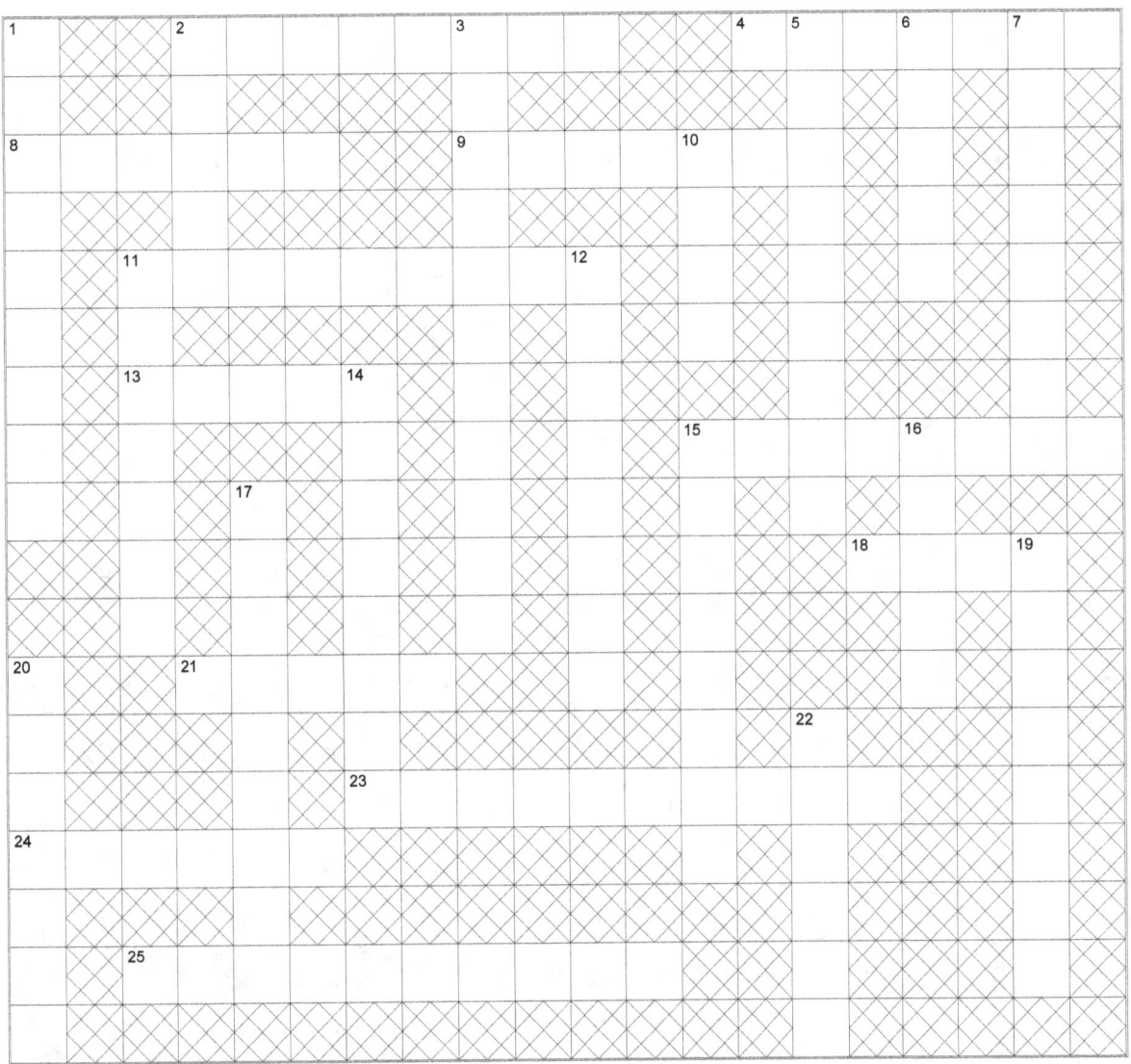

Across

2. An agent sent to represent or advance the interests of another
4. Seriously
8. Commotion; riot
9. Threatening
11. Necessary requirement
13. A contest between antagonists; a match
15. Understandable; clear
18. Disgusting; loathsome
21. Produced; fathered
23. An observer of an event
24. Youthful; immature
25. Inharmonious; conflicting

Down

1. Exclude from public favor
2. Avoid; evade
3. Detestable things
5. Elastic; able to spring back
6. Courage and boldness, as in battle; bravery
7. Lacking in spirit or energy
10. Prophetic sign
11. Criticized or reproved sharply; reprimanded
12. A spiritual or incorporeal entity
14. Seemingly reliable but incorrect
15. Maim
16. To represent falsely; pretend to
17. Arrogantly domineering or overbearing
19. Expressive; persuasive
20. Distinguish; perceive
22. A state of violent mental agitation or wild excitement

Things Fall Apart Vocabulary Crossword 3 Answer Key

Across
- 2. An agent sent to represent or advance the interests of another
- 4. Seriously
- 8. Commotion; riot
- 9. Threatening
- 11. Necessary requirement
- 13. A contest between antagonists; a match
- 15. Understandable; clear
- 18. Disgusting; loathsome
- 21. Produced; fathered
- 23. An observer of an event
- 24. Youthful; immature
- 25. Inharmonious; conflicting

Down
- 1. Exclude from public favor
- 2. Avoid; evade
- 3. Detestable things
- 5. Elastic; able to spring back
- 6. Courage and boldness, as in battle; bravery
- 7. Lacking in spirit or energy
- 10. Prophetic sign
- 11. Criticized or reproved sharply; reprimanded
- 12. A spiritual or incorporeal entity
- 14. Seemingly reliable but incorrect
- 15. Maim
- 16. To represent falsely; pretend to
- 17. Arrogantly domineering or overbearing
- 19. Expressive; persuasive
- 20. Distinguish; perceive
- 22. A state of violent mental agitation or wild excitement

Things Fall Apart Vocabulary Crossword 4

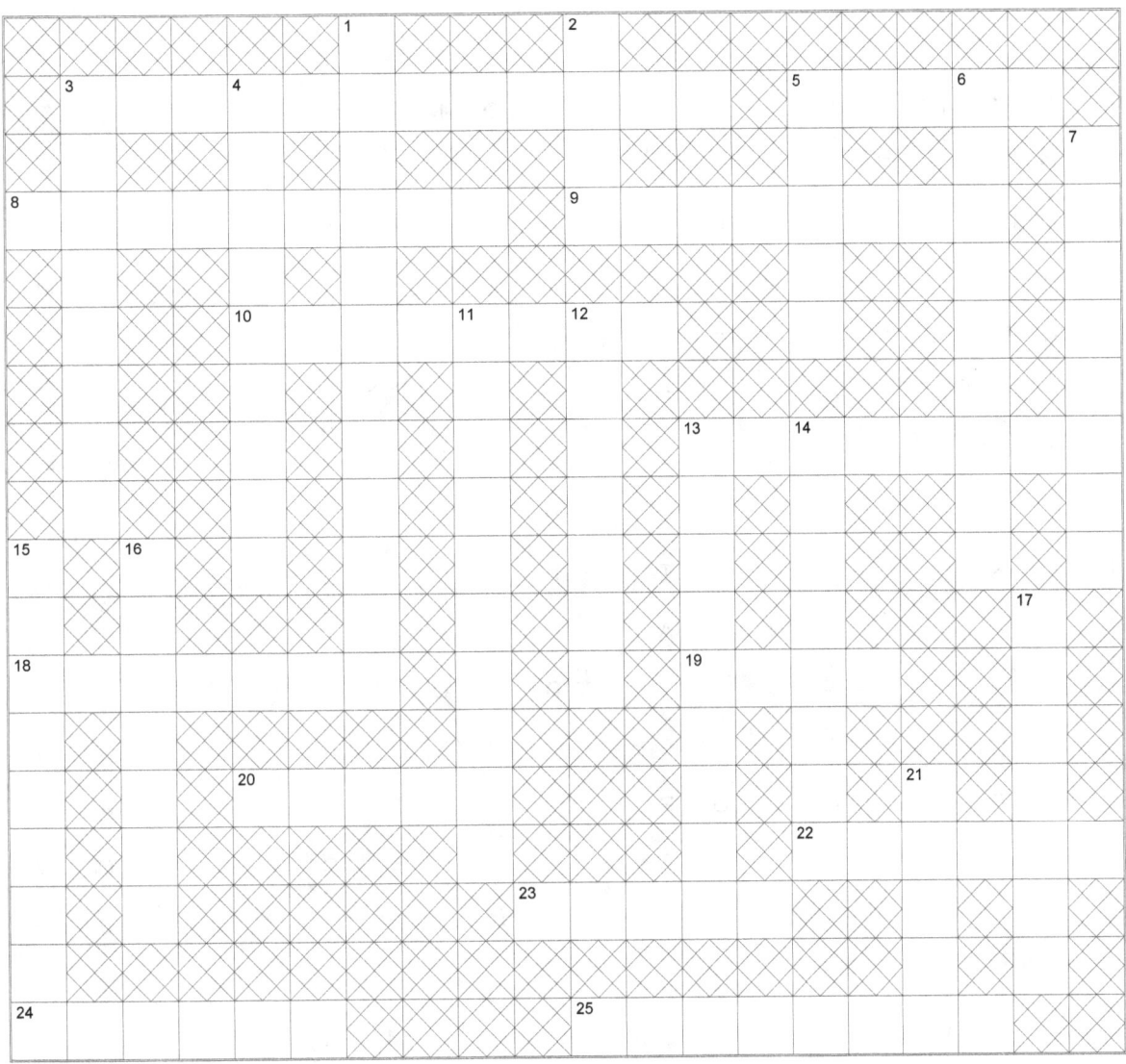

Across
3. Payment or reimbursement
5. Produced; fathered
8. Arrogantly domineering or overbearing
9. Expressive; persuasive
10. An agent sent to represent or advance the interests of another
13. Impression produced by achievement or reputation
18. Skill in deception; guile
19. Prophetic sign
20. Courage and boldness, as in battle; bravery
22. Youthful; immature
23. To represent falsely; pretend to
24. Commotion; riot
25. Stirred up; disturbed

Down
1. Stimulating or exciting
2. Disgusting; loathsome
3. Of a group of people
4. Lasting for eternity
5. A contest between antagonists; a match
6. Exclude from public favor
7. Impending; near at hand
11. An observer of an event
12. Criticized or reproved sharply; reprimanded
13. Angering; causing retaliation
14. Known only to the chosen few
15. Beginning to exist or appear
16. Related to a clan or tribe
17. Threadlike
21. Avoid; evade

Things Fall Apart Vocabulary Crossword 4 Answer Key

Across
3. Payment or reimbursement
5. Produced; fathered
8. Arrogantly domineering or overbearing
9. Expressive; persuasive
10. An agent sent to represent or advance the interests of another
13. Impression produced by achievement or reputation
18. Skill in deception; guile
19. Prophetic sign
20. Courage and boldness, as in battle; bravery
22. Youthful; immature
23. To represent falsely; pretend to
24. Commotion; riot
25. Stirred up; disturbed

Down
1. Stimulating or exciting
2. Disgusting; loathsome
3. Of a group of people
4. Lasting for eternity
5. A contest between antagonists; a match
6. Exclude from public favor
7. Impending; near at hand
11. An observer of an event
12. Criticized or reproved sharply; reprimanded
13. Angering; causing retaliation
14. Known only to the chosen few
15. Beginning to exist or appear
16. Related to a clan or tribe
17. Threadlike
21. Avoid; evade

Things Fall Apart Vocabulary Juggle Letters 1

1. NMEMNIIT = 1. _____
   Impending; near at hand

2. IMTOIANBOAN = 2. _____
   Detestable things

3. YOCPOSULI = 3. _____
   Abundantly

4. NOISSCTOOALN = 4. _____
   Words of comfort

5. OUSROIONT = 5. _____
   Known widely and usually unfavorably

6. LNALEMEOVCE = 6. _____
   Evil or harmful influence

7. ADGAHRG = 7. _____
   Appearing worn and exhausted

8. EQENTUOL = 8. _____
   Expressive; persuasive

9. OADPNEUNMMI = 9. _____
   Wild tumult

10. SOROCEPUM =10. _____
    Mental calmness

11. IICTINEPN =11. _____
    Beginning to exist or appear

12. OMCNACDIATMOO =12. _____
    Help; adaptation

13. OCMERMPSIO =13. _____
    Adjustment

14. BRERDPTUE =14. _____
    Greatly disturbed

15. UTIAMTLE =15. _____
    Maim

Things Fall Apart Vocabulary Juggle Letters 1 Answer Key

1. NMEMNIIT = 1. IMMINENT
Impending; near at hand

2. IMTOIANBOAN = 2. ABOMINATION
Detestable things

3. YOCPOSULI = 3. COPIOUSLY
Abundantly

4. NOISSCTOOALN = 4. CONSOLATIONS
Words of comfort

5. OUSROIONT = 5. NOTORIOUS
Known widely and usually unfavorably

6. LNALEMEOVCE = 6. MALEVOLENCE
Evil or harmful influence

7. ADGAHRG = 7. HAGGARD
Appearing worn and exhausted

8. EQENTUOL = 8. ELOQUENT
Expressive; persuasive

9. OADPNEUNMMI = 9. PANDEMONIUM
Wild tumult

10. SOROCEPUM =10. COMPOSURE
Mental calmness

11. IICTINEPN =11. INCIPIENT
Beginning to exist or appear

12. OMCNACDIATMOO =12. ACCOMMODATION
Help; adaptation

13. OCMERMPSIO =13. COMPROMISE
Adjustment

14. BRERDPTUE =14. PERTURBED
Greatly disturbed

15. UTIAMTLE =15. MUTILATE
Maim

Things Fall Apart Vocabulary Juggle Letters 2

1. SOOIOTNUR = 1. _____
   Known widely and usually unfavorably

2. EIIEVRDS = 2. _____
   Ridiculing

3. RDUPEETBR = 3. _____
   Greatly disturbed

4. DSEIFFDU = 4. _____
   Spread in all directions

5. EIEGPTSR = 5. _____
   Impression produced by achievement or reputation

6. NNCGUIN = 6. _____
   Skill in deception; guile

7. TCORESIE = 7. _____
   Known only to the chosen few

8. SIOYOCUPL = 8. _____
   Abundantly

9. TITAGDEA = 9. _____
   Stirred up; disturbed

10. SAITROGENNI =10. _____
    Unresisting; patiently submissive

11. NIEPTIINC =11. _____
    Beginning to exist or appear

12. SLSLSEIT =12. _____
    Lacking in spirit or energy

13. NRIDEKD =13. _____
    Related to a clan or tribe

14. IEITQURSE =14. _____
    Necessary requirement

15. NPVIMRETDIO =15. _____
    Not providing for the future; thriftless; incautious

Things Fall Apart Vocabulary Juggle Letters 2 Answer Key

1. SOOIOTNUR = 1. NOTORIOUS
   Known widely and usually unfavorably

2. EIIEVRDS = 2. DERISIVE
   Ridiculing

3. RDUPEETBR = 3. PERTURBED
   Greatly disturbed

4. DSEIFFDU = 4. DIFFUSED
   Spread in all directions

5. EIEGPTSR = 5. PRESTIGE
   Impression produced by achievement or reputation

6. NNCGUIN = 6. CUNNING
   Skill in deception; guile

7. TCORESIE = 7. ESOTERIC
   Known only to the chosen few

8. SIOYOCUPL = 8. COPIOUSLY
   Abundantly

9. TITAGDEA = 9. AGITATED
   Stirred up; disturbed

10. SAITROGENNI = 10. RESIGNATION
    Unresisting; patiently submissive

11. NIEPTIINC = 11. INCIPIENT
    Beginning to exist or appear

12. SLSLSEIT = 12. LISTLESS
    Lacking in spirit or energy

13. NRIDEKD = 13. KINDRED
    Related to a clan or tribe

14. IEITQURSE = 14. REQUISITE
    Necessary requirement

15. NPVIMRETDIO = 15. IMPROVIDENT
    Not providing for the future; thriftless; incautious

Things Fall Apart Vocabulary Juggle Letters 3

1. CNREDSI = 1. _____
   Distinguish; perceive

2. DUBKREE = 2. _____
   Criticized or reproved sharply; reprimanded

3. MUOAMLNC = 3. _____
   Of a group of people

4. EVLI = 4. _____
   Disgusting; loathsome

5. DDSIOANTCR = 5. _____
   Inharmonious; conflicting

6. INEGF = 6. _____
   To represent falsely; pretend to

7. DAGGARH = 7. _____
   Appearing worn and exhausted

8. NTIIIPNEC = 8. _____
   Beginning to exist or appear

9. IVSEDEIR = 9. _____
   Ridiculing

10. VNISTELAR = 10. _____
    Amount of time between specified instances

11. REIPIUSMO = 11. _____
    Arrogantly domineering or overbearing

12. LAOCEEEMVLN = 12. _____
    Evil or harmful influence

13. ENSUTTD = 13. _____
    Having growth or development stopped

14. YIMRSASE = 14. _____
    An agent sent to represent or advance the interests of another

15. ORVLA = 15. _____
    Courage and boldness, as in battle; bravery

Things Fall Apart Vocabulary Juggle Letters 3 Answer Key

1. CNREDSI = 1. DISCERN
Distinguish; perceive

2. DUBKREE = 2. REBUKED
Criticized or reproved sharply; reprimanded

3. MUOAMLNC = 3. COMMUNAL
Of a group of people

4. EVLI = 4. VILE
Disgusting; loathsome

5. DDSIOANTCR = 5. DISCORDANT
Inharmonious; conflicting

6. INEGF = 6. FEIGN
To represent falsely; pretend to

7. DAGGARH = 7. HAGGARD
Appearing worn and exhausted

8. NTIIIPNEC = 8. INCIPIENT
Beginning to exist or appear

9. IVSEDEIR = 9. DERISIVE
Ridiculing

10. VNISTELAR = 10. INTERVALS
Amount of time between specified instances

11. REIPIUSMO = 11. IMPERIOUS
Arrogantly domineering or overbearing

12. LAOCEEEMVLN = 12. MALEVOLENCE
Evil or harmful influence

13. ENSUTTD = 13. STUNTED
Having growth or development stopped

14. YIMRSASE = 14. EMISSARY
An agent sent to represent or advance the interests of another

15. ORVLA = 15. VALOR
Courage and boldness, as in battle; bravery

Things Fall Apart Vocabulary Juggle Letters 4

1. LEISLSST = 1. _____
   Lacking in spirit or energy

2. INOUSMO = 2. _____
   Threatening

3. UODOPFRN = 3. _____
   Deep; complete

4. PIOESUSC = 4. _____
   Seemingly reliable but incorrect

5. OOCTACAIDNMMO = 5. _____
   Help; adaptation

6. MTLTUU = 6. _____
   Commotion; riot

7. EEITRQIUS = 7. _____
   Necessary requirement

8. CXTAOINGITNI = 8. _____
   Stimulating or exciting

9. CEAOLLVEEMN = 9. _____
   Evil or harmful influence

10. TIMELTAU =10. _____
    Maim

11. ERNKIDD =11. _____
    Related to a clan or tribe

12. ROUMPIIES =12. _____
    Arrogantly domineering or overbearing

13. UDRBKEE =13. _____
    Criticized or reproved sharply; reprimanded

14. NAIOPPRBTAO =14. _____
    Approval

15. ONEEETLNBV =15. _____
    Characterized by or suggestive of doing good

Things Fall Apart Vocabulary Juggle Letters 4 Answer Key

1. LEISLSST = 1. LISTLESS
Lacking in spirit or energy

2. INOUSMO = 2. OMINOUS
Threatening

3. UODOPFRN = 3. PROFOUND
Deep; complete

4. PIOESUSC = 4. SPECIOUS
Seemingly reliable but incorrect

5. OOCTACAIDNMMO = 5. ACCOMMODATION
Help; adaptation

6. MTLTUU = 6. TUMULT
Commotion; riot

7. EEITRQIUS = 7. REQUISITE
Necessary requirement

8. CXTAOINGITNI = 8. INTOXICATING
Stimulating or exciting

9. CEAOLLVEEMN = 9. MALEVOLENCE
Evil or harmful influence

10. TIMELTAU =10. MUTILATE
Maim

11. ERNKIDD =11. KINDRED
Related to a clan or tribe

12. ROUMPIIES =12. IMPERIOUS
Arrogantly domineering or overbearing

13. UDRBKEE =13. REBUKED
Criticized or reproved sharply; reprimanded

14. NAIOPPRBTAO =14. APPROBATION
Approval

15. ONEEETLNBV =15. BENEVOLENT
Characterized by or suggestive of doing good

ABOMINATION	Detestable things
ACCOMMODATION	Help; adaptation
AGITATED	Stirred up; disturbed
APPROBATION	Approval
BEGOT	Produced; fathered
BENEVOLENT	Characterized by or suggestive of doing good
BOUTS	A contest between antagonists; a match

BRUSQUENESS	Abrupt and curt in manner or speech; discourteously blunt
CALABASHES	Utensils or containers made from dried gourds
CALLOW	Youthful; immature
CAPRICIOUS	Impulsive and unpredictable
COMMUNAL	Of a group of people
COMPENSATION	Payment or reimbursement
COMPOSURE	Mental calmness

COMPROMISE	Adjustment
CONSOLATIONS	Words of comfort
COPIOUSLY	Abundantly
CUNNING	Skill in deception; guile
DELECTABLE	Delightful; delicious
DERISIVE	Ridiculing
DIFFUSED	Spread in all directions

DISCERN	Distinguish; perceive
DISCORDANT	Inharmonious; conflicting
ELOQUENT	Expressive; persuasive
ELUDE	Avoid; evade
EMANATION	Issuing forth
EMISSARY	An agent sent to represent or advance the interests of another
ESOTERIC	Known only to the chosen few

ESSENCES	A spiritual or incorporeal entity
FEIGN	To represent falsely; pretend to
FIBROUS	Threadlike
FLOURISH	Grow well; prosper
FRENZY	A state of violent mental agitation or wild excitement
GRAVELY	Seriously
HAGGARD	Appearing worn and exhausted

HARBINGERS	One that indicates or foreshadows what is to come; a forerunner
IMMINENT	Impending; near at hand
IMPENETRABLY	Not able to be entered or pierced
IMPERIOUS	Arrogantly domineering or overbearing
IMPROVIDENT	Not providing for the future; thriftless; incautious
INCIPIENT	Beginning to exist or appear
INTERVALS	Amount of time between specified instances

INTOXICATING	Stimulating or exciting
KINDRED	Related to a clan or tribe
LISTLESS	Lacking in spirit or energy
MALEVOLENCE	Evil or harmful influence
MANIFEST	Understandable; clear
MIRTHLESS	Without laughter
MISCREANT	Wretch; villain

MUTILATE	Maim
NOTORIOUS	Known widely and usually unfavorably
OMEN	Prophetic sign
OMINOUS	Threatening
OSTRACIZE	Exclude from public favor
PANDEMONIUM	Wild tumult
PERPETUAL	Lasting for eternity

PERTURBED	Greatly disturbed
PRESTIGE	Impression produced by achievement or reputation
PROFOUND	Deep; complete
PROVOKING	Angering; causing retaliation
REBUKED	Criticized or reproved sharply; reprimanded
REQUISITE	Necessary requirement
RESIGNATION	Unresisting; patiently submissive

RESILIENT	Elastic; able to spring back
SPECIOUS	Seemingly reliable but incorrect
SPECTATORS	An observer of an event
STUNTED	Having growth or development stopped
TUMULT	Commotion; riot
VALOR	Courage and boldness, as in battle; bravery
VILE	Disgusting; loathsome

Things Fall Apart Vocabulary

FLOURISH	INCIPIENT	EMISSARY	CALLOW	APPROBATION
REQUISITE	MISCREANT	TUMULT	COMMUNAL	NOTORIOUS
ELOQUENT	GRAVELY	FREE SPACE	INTERVALS	REBUKED
PRESTIGE	BEGOT	IMPERIOUS	IMPENETRABLY	BRUSQUENESS
IMPROVIDENT	VALOR	FRENZY	RESIGNATION	DERISIVE

Things Fall Apart Vocabulary

PERTURBED	OMINOUS	KINDRED	ESOTERIC	DISCERN
CONSOLATIONS	PANDEMONIUM	PERPETUAL	COPIOUSLY	BOUTS
FEIGN	OSTRACIZE	FREE SPACE	DISCORDANT	INTOXICATING
IMMINENT	OMEN	PROVOKING	ESSENCES	ABOMINATION
STUNTED	SPECIOUS	CUNNING	VILE	HARBINGERS

Things Fall Apart Vocabulary

MALEVOLENCE	OMINOUS	MIRTHLESS	APPROBATION	DISCERN
DISCORDANT	PERPETUAL	ELOQUENT	DIFFUSED	SPECIOUS
IMPERIOUS	COMMUNAL	FREE SPACE	FRENZY	COMPOSURE
FLOURISH	IMMINENT	INTERVALS	TUMULT	CONSOLATIONS
HAGGARD	PROVOKING	AGITATED	RESIGNATION	BRUSQUENESS

Things Fall Apart Vocabulary

BENEVOLENT	INCIPIENT	DELECTABLE	COMPENSATION	INTOXICATING
RESILIENT	LISTLESS	IMPENETRABLY	FEIGN	PRESTIGE
GRAVELY	BEGOT	FREE SPACE	REQUISITE	COPIOUSLY
ESSENCES	FIBROUS	PERTURBED	DERISIVE	MANIFEST
OMEN	STUNTED	REBUKED	BOUTS	CUNNING

Things Fall Apart Vocabulary

NOTORIOUS	PANDEMONIUM	PROVOKING	PERPETUAL	OSTRACIZE
DELECTABLE	GRAVELY	KINDRED	IMMINENT	ESOTERIC
IMPERIOUS	BRUSQUENESS	FREE SPACE	FEIGN	HARBINGERS
COPIOUSLY	DISCORDANT	IMPROVIDENT	VALOR	INCIPIENT
DERISIVE	EMISSARY	OMINOUS	COMPENSATION	ACCOMMODATION

Things Fall Apart Vocabulary

ABOMINATION	MANIFEST	VILE	BENEVOLENT	HAGGARD
EMANATION	ESSENCES	CUNNING	COMPOSURE	CAPRICIOUS
BEGOT	STUNTED	FREE SPACE	PRESTIGE	FIBROUS
FRENZY	DIFFUSED	CONSOLATIONS	SPECIOUS	COMMUNAL
REQUISITE	APPROBATION	MALEVOLENCE	MIRTHLESS	DISCERN

Things Fall Apart Vocabulary

MISCREANT	DISCORDANT	BEGOT	APPROBATION	BOUTS
BRUSQUENESS	CALLOW	COMPOSURE	DELECTABLE	KINDRED
OSTRACIZE	PROFOUND	FREE SPACE	DERISIVE	NOTORIOUS
INTOXICATING	STUNTED	HARBINGERS	IMPENETRABLY	PRESTIGE
MIRTHLESS	PROVOKING	CALABASHES	CONSOLATIONS	OMINOUS

Things Fall Apart Vocabulary

PANDEMONIUM	TUMULT	COPIOUSLY	REQUISITE	VILE
EMANATION	FEIGN	EMISSARY	VALOR	DIFFUSED
PERTURBED	MALEVOLENCE	FREE SPACE	GRAVELY	ABOMINATION
ELOQUENT	FLOURISH	COMPENSATION	ELUDE	OMEN
INCIPIENT	MANIFEST	INTERVALS	SPECTATORS	ESSENCES

Things Fall Apart Vocabulary

SPECIOUS	ESOTERIC	OSTRACIZE	BENEVOLENT	PRESTIGE
CUNNING	EMISSARY	EMANATION	PROFOUND	STUNTED
DISCERN	COPIOUSLY	FREE SPACE	AGITATED	PERPETUAL
NOTORIOUS	ELOQUENT	MALEVOLENCE	INTOXICATING	CONSOLATIONS
OMINOUS	ACCOMMODATION	FEIGN	COMMUNAL	PERTURBED

Things Fall Apart Vocabulary

GRAVELY	PROVOKING	VILE	CAPRICIOUS	IMPROVIDENT
INCIPIENT	ABOMINATION	INTERVALS	BRUSQUENESS	COMPENSATION
CALABASHES	HAGGARD	FREE SPACE	ELUDE	FLOURISH
MANIFEST	HARBINGERS	SPECTATORS	VALOR	IMPENETRABLY
FIBROUS	KINDRED	MISCREANT	PANDEMONIUM	BOUTS

Things Fall Apart Vocabulary

IMPROVIDENT	PANDEMONIUM	FIBROUS	PROVOKING	SPECIOUS
INCIPIENT	CAPRICIOUS	COMPROMISE	OSTRACIZE	DIFFUSED
VILE	BOUTS	FREE SPACE	MANIFEST	EMISSARY
ELUDE	PROFOUND	CUNNING	MUTILATE	DERISIVE
STUNTED	EMANATION	IMPENETRABLY	AGITATED	DISCERN

Things Fall Apart Vocabulary

KINDRED	COMPENSATION	HAGGARD	NOTORIOUS	TUMULT
COPIOUSLY	GRAVELY	MIRTHLESS	INTERVALS	RESIGNATION
CONSOLATIONS	FEIGN	FREE SPACE	COMMUNAL	PRESTIGE
OMEN	MALEVOLENCE	CALABASHES	BENEVOLENT	SPECTATORS
DISCORDANT	INTOXICATING	REBUKED	OMINOUS	ESSENCES

Things Fall Apart Vocabulary

FRENZY	PROFOUND	APPROBATION	HARBINGERS	RESIGNATION
SPECIOUS	BENEVOLENT	HAGGARD	REBUKED	CALLOW
COMPENSATION	PRESTIGE	FREE SPACE	DIFFUSED	CONSOLATIONS
IMPENETRABLY	CAPRICIOUS	DERISIVE	NOTORIOUS	FIBROUS
PERTURBED	EMANATION	FLOURISH	DISCORDANT	MISCREANT

Things Fall Apart Vocabulary

ELOQUENT	IMPERIOUS	CALABASHES	OSTRACIZE	OMEN
BEGOT	ESOTERIC	COMPOSURE	STUNTED	VILE
BRUSQUENESS	COMMUNAL	FREE SPACE	ELUDE	LISTLESS
EMISSARY	DELECTABLE	VALOR	CUNNING	ACCOMMODATION
MUTILATE	MALEVOLENCE	TUMULT	COPIOUSLY	INCIPIENT

Things Fall Apart Vocabulary

GRAVELY	CONSOLATIONS	MALEVOLENCE	PERPETUAL	ELOQUENT
PROFOUND	HARBINGERS	COMPOSURE	RESIGNATION	FIBROUS
MIRTHLESS	INTOXICATING	FREE SPACE	SPECTATORS	BEGOT
VALOR	DELECTABLE	STUNTED	CALLOW	IMPERIOUS
KINDRED	PROVOKING	APPROBATION	RESILIENT	DISCORDANT

Things Fall Apart Vocabulary

SPECIOUS	REBUKED	BENEVOLENT	MANIFEST	MISCREANT
COMPROMISE	LISTLESS	EMISSARY	FLOURISH	DIFFUSED
CUNNING	FEIGN	FREE SPACE	PRESTIGE	VILE
EMANATION	ACCOMMODATION	DISCERN	ESOTERIC	ABOMINATION
INCIPIENT	DERISIVE	ELUDE	CAPRICIOUS	INTERVALS

Things Fall Apart Vocabulary

VALOR	COMMUNAL	CALLOW	BOUTS	RESILIENT
PANDEMONIUM	EMANATION	MIRTHLESS	IMPROVIDENT	PRESTIGE
COMPOSURE	FEIGN	FREE SPACE	ACCOMMODATION	DIFFUSED
MUTILATE	PERPETUAL	DERISIVE	OMINOUS	REQUISITE
EMISSARY	PERTURBED	COMPENSATION	CAPRICIOUS	TUMULT

Things Fall Apart Vocabulary

DISCORDANT	LISTLESS	APPROBATION	PROVOKING	ELOQUENT
INTOXICATING	INCIPIENT	GRAVELY	COPIOUSLY	BRUSQUENESS
CUNNING	ESSENCES	FREE SPACE	FIBROUS	SPECIOUS
MALEVOLENCE	RESIGNATION	CALABASHES	PROFOUND	CONSOLATIONS
NOTORIOUS	KINDRED	ELUDE	FLOURISH	FRENZY

Things Fall Apart Vocabulary

ESOTERIC	BRUSQUENESS	EMISSARY	PRESTIGE	LISTLESS
COMPROMISE	INTOXICATING	VILE	PROVOKING	MANIFEST
BOUTS	REQUISITE	FREE SPACE	INTERVALS	STUNTED
PERPETUAL	CONSOLATIONS	FEIGN	MUTILATE	APPROBATION
FRENZY	ABOMINATION	IMPERIOUS	DIFFUSED	SPECTATORS

Things Fall Apart Vocabulary

HARBINGERS	PANDEMONIUM	IMPENETRABLY	CALLOW	AGITATED
ACCOMMODATION	OSTRACIZE	DISCERN	COMPOSURE	CAPRICIOUS
NOTORIOUS	PROFOUND	FREE SPACE	ELOQUENT	IMMINENT
IMPROVIDENT	VALOR	DISCORDANT	OMINOUS	HAGGARD
RESILIENT	DERISIVE	COMMUNAL	DELECTABLE	CALABASHES

Things Fall Apart Vocabulary

MANIFEST	VALOR	ELUDE	INTERVALS	COMPENSATION
DELECTABLE	COPIOUSLY	FEIGN	PERPETUAL	FRENZY
ESSENCES	AGITATED	FREE SPACE	HAGGARD	PANDEMONIUM
LISTLESS	VILE	ELOQUENT	DERISIVE	FIBROUS
FLOURISH	ESOTERIC	SPECTATORS	MUTILATE	APPROBATION

Things Fall Apart Vocabulary

IMPERIOUS	PRESTIGE	RESIGNATION	PROVOKING	CALABASHES
GRAVELY	PERTURBED	INTOXICATING	EMANATION	OMINOUS
COMPOSURE	OSTRACIZE	FREE SPACE	EMISSARY	PROFOUND
DISCORDANT	HARBINGERS	CONSOLATIONS	CALLOW	IMPROVIDENT
ACCOMMODATION	OMEN	ABOMINATION	CAPRICIOUS	MALEVOLENCE

Things Fall Apart Vocabulary

ELUDE	HAGGARD	SPECIOUS	BRUSQUENESS	ABOMINATION
IMMINENT	MUTILATE	OMEN	HARBINGERS	IMPENETRABLY
EMISSARY	FRENZY	FREE SPACE	TUMULT	APPROBATION
PERTURBED	RESIGNATION	RESILIENT	COPIOUSLY	GRAVELY
DISCORDANT	DISCERN	FIBROUS	COMPENSATION	CALABASHES

Things Fall Apart Vocabulary

FEIGN	OMINOUS	STUNTED	EMANATION	KINDRED
MIRTHLESS	NOTORIOUS	DERISIVE	PERPETUAL	VALOR
SPECTATORS	CONSOLATIONS	FREE SPACE	REQUISITE	COMPROMISE
CAPRICIOUS	LISTLESS	AGITATED	DIFFUSED	PRESTIGE
ESSENCES	COMPOSURE	OSTRACIZE	MISCREANT	DELECTABLE

Things Fall Apart Vocabulary

PANDEMONIUM	BOUTS	LISTLESS	MISCREANT	OMINOUS
STUNTED	FEIGN	ELUDE	INTERVALS	HARBINGERS
AGITATED	FLOURISH	FREE SPACE	IMPENETRABLY	DISCORDANT
CONSOLATIONS	FIBROUS	BEGOT	VILE	COMPENSATION
RESIGNATION	SPECTATORS	DERISIVE	INTOXICATING	EMISSARY

Things Fall Apart Vocabulary

CALABASHES	DISCERN	OMEN	PRESTIGE	ACCOMMODATION
MALEVOLENCE	FRENZY	PERPETUAL	MIRTHLESS	REBUKED
GRAVELY	CAPRICIOUS	FREE SPACE	PROFOUND	BENEVOLENT
BRUSQUENESS	PERTURBED	HAGGARD	ABOMINATION	MUTILATE
ESOTERIC	IMPERIOUS	CALLOW	OSTRACIZE	TUMULT

Things Fall Apart Vocabulary

DIFFUSED	BOUTS	FEIGN	TUMULT	ELUDE
COMMUNAL	IMPROVIDENT	GRAVELY	AGITATED	DELECTABLE
SPECTATORS	HARBINGERS	FREE SPACE	STUNTED	MIRTHLESS
INTOXICATING	BEGOT	MALEVOLENCE	DERISIVE	RESILIENT
NOTORIOUS	IMPENETRABLY	COPIOUSLY	DISCORDANT	PERTURBED

Things Fall Apart Vocabulary

CALABASHES	PANDEMONIUM	BRUSQUENESS	CONSOLATIONS	IMMINENT
BENEVOLENT	REQUISITE	DISCERN	PROFOUND	PROVOKING
COMPOSURE	INCIPIENT	FREE SPACE	MUTILATE	OMINOUS
CALLOW	LISTLESS	INTERVALS	VILE	APPROBATION
PRESTIGE	ACCOMMODATION	RESIGNATION	HAGGARD	CAPRICIOUS

Things Fall Apart Vocabulary

PANDEMONIUM	IMPROVIDENT	STUNTED	NOTORIOUS	KINDRED
COMPENSATION	AGITATED	IMPERIOUS	HAGGARD	IMPENETRABLY
REQUISITE	PROVOKING	FREE SPACE	SPECTATORS	DELECTABLE
ESSENCES	PERPETUAL	INTERVALS	ESOTERIC	RESILIENT
VALOR	VILE	CONSOLATIONS	CALABASHES	INCIPIENT

Things Fall Apart Vocabulary

PROFOUND	DISCERN	ELUDE	EMANATION	COMPOSURE
CUNNING	OMINOUS	RESIGNATION	BRUSQUENESS	OSTRACIZE
HARBINGERS	GRAVELY	FREE SPACE	FEIGN	COMPROMISE
CALLOW	ACCOMMODATION	PERTURBED	APPROBATION	MALEVOLENCE
BENEVOLENT	ABOMINATION	INTOXICATING	ELOQUENT	FRENZY

Things Fall Apart Vocabulary

VILE	BOUTS	MALEVOLENCE	BRUSQUENESS	ACCOMMODATION
MIRTHLESS	SPECIOUS	REQUISITE	OSTRACIZE	APPROBATION
VALOR	PRESTIGE	FREE SPACE	MANIFEST	PERPETUAL
DELECTABLE	MUTILATE	KINDRED	FIBROUS	CUNNING
PERTURBED	DERISIVE	PANDEMONIUM	IMPERIOUS	FEIGN

Things Fall Apart Vocabulary

INTERVALS	RESILIENT	FLOURISH	IMPROVIDENT	ESSENCES
COMMUNAL	ELUDE	RESIGNATION	SPECTATORS	INCIPIENT
PROFOUND	GRAVELY	FREE SPACE	EMISSARY	COPIOUSLY
CALABASHES	DISCORDANT	NOTORIOUS	CONSOLATIONS	PROVOKING
BEGOT	ELOQUENT	HAGGARD	COMPOSURE	HARBINGERS

www.ingramcontent.com/pod-product-compliance
Lightning Source LLC
Chambersburg PA
CBHW081455070526
44586CB00019B/2366